Confessions of the Pastor's Wife

SARA M. SNYDER

Confessions of the Pastor's Wife

©2015 Sara M. Snyder

Notice of Rights

Manufactured in the United States of America. No part of this book may be reproduced, transmitted in any form or by any means—electronic, or mechanical—including photocopying and recording, or by any information storage or retrieval system, except as may be expressly permitted in writing by the publisher or author.

Notice of Liability

The information in this book is distributed on an "as is" basis, for informational purposes only, without warranty. While every precaution has been taken in the production of this book, neither the copyright owner nor the publisher shall have any liability to any person or entity with respect to any liability, loss, or damage caused or alleged to be caused directly or indirectly by the information contained in this book.

ISBN-13: 9781937660819

Ebook ISBN: 9781937660826

Published By:
Sara M. Snyder

*To my parents, for giving me
the tools to dream.*

*To my husband, for helping me
make that dream a reality.*

Sara M. Snyder
12/2021

Table Of Contents

Introduction 1
You ARE ~~Good~~ Enough 3
Why Hiding Out Is Not an Option 7
Accepting Change 11
I Will Remember 15
Stormy Days 19
Swimming into the Waves 23
When You're Just Not Feeling the Faithfulness 27
Forget the Hustle 31
Lay it Down 35
Building Consistency 39
Imperfect Perfection 43
When Life Feels Like a Roller Coaster 47
Embracing Your Gifts 51
When the Future Is Scary and Uncertain 55
God is Not a GPS 59
Calla Lilly Grace 63
Wait and See 67
Hemmed In 71
Seeing God in the Midst of an Epic Fail 75
Being an Active Listener 79
Seed-Planting Days 83
The Mighty Oaks 87
Bird Feeder Transformation 91

Kitchen Renovations	95
Pressing On	99
Don't Try So Hard	103
Free Falling with God	107
Do What You're Supposed to Do	111
Little Signs	115
Faith and Trust	119
Legacies	123
A Bit of Dirt	127
Road Construction	131
An Air-Tight Seal	135
Undone	139
Slogging Through the Wilderness	143
Missing the Mark By An Inch	147
Ask for Help	151
Taco Tuesdays	155
Accepting God's Call	159
Hearing God's Call	165
Wonder Moments	169
The Nature of Gratitude	173
Being a Faith Warrior	177
Pray	181
Single-Minded Focus	185
I'm Going With You	189
When Enough Is…Enough	193
Abiding in Surrender	197
Holding Together	203
Be Yourself	207
Ordinary Time	211

Acknowledgements

One of the central truths of life is that none of us can accomplish anything on our own. We were created to need others. This is the place where I get to tell you about the people who really made this book possible.

My family: From encouragement, faith, and inspiration to advice, critique, and wisdom, my family has done it all. They build me up, cheer me on, and pick up the pieces when it all falls apart.

My husband, Chris: My husband and I truly have a yin-yang relationship. Where I am impulsive and big-picture oriented, he is logical and takes care of all the details. He is the one who stops me from making business deals that involve accepting lattes instead of cash. I never would have gotten here had it not been for him.

My teachers: I love teaching because I had great teachers. Thank you for pushing me, for encouraging me, and for giving me knowledge.

My first great teacher was my dad. He encouraged me to think for myself, to seek out knowledge, and to always ask questions. Mrs. Rife was "the Queen of Everything." She took a nerdy, awkward middle schooler and turned her into her "princess." Teachers truly can change lives—make sure to show them some love.

My favorite writers: Before I loved writing, I loved reading. I have been inspired by so many great works—from Judy Blume to Anne Lamott, writers have helped to shape my thinking, my beliefs, and my understanding of myself.

My publishing team: I could not publish a book on my own. There are way too many details involved, and I'm really not technically savvy. Thank you Hanne Moon and Heritage Press for getting it all right. Thank you, too, to Lisa Thomson at BZ Studio for the incredible design work.

Confessions of the Pastor's Wife

INTRODUCTION

This book is not an exposé of ministry life. I'm sorry if that disappoints you. After eleven years as a pastor's wife, there are many stories I could tell. Some of them are funny. Some are sad. Some are full of wonder and beauty. And some are still painful to the touch. I expect that most of you have similar stories to share. And that, my friends, is the point of this book.

My great big confession to you is that I am you. Well, obviously not you—there's only one you. But my life, like your life, is full of many different stories.

Like many of you, I am a wife. I am a working mother. I struggle with the same issues of confidence, purpose, and identity that many of you struggle with. I make mistakes—sometimes really big ones. But permeating through all of that is a deeply rooted love of God and an intrinsic desire to draw closer to him. That's what this book is really about. It's a three-way conversation between me, you, and God as we journey to a place of deeper faith—a place of authentic faith. And that authentic faith begins with a confession—the confession that we don't have it all together, our lives aren't perfect, and we need God to love us, forgive us, guide us, and redeem us.

There are fifty-two devotionals in this book—one for each week of the year. These devotions reflect the ways in which God has spoken (and is speaking) to me as I work toward building an authentic faith. My prayer is that as you read each devotion, you will find a bit of your own story there. I pray that God will reach

Confessions of the Pastor's Wife

beyond the words on the page and lay his hand directly on your heart so that you will know him more.

Here is the prayer I always pray before entering into the study of God's word. May it open the door for the Holy Spirit to enter into your life and illuminate all that God has to say to you.

Dear God,

Please guide and direct my reading of your Word and my time with you. Let your Holy Spirit guide my thoughts and grant me a word that I may take with me into today.

In Jesus Name, Amen

Blessings and Peace,
Sara

Confessions of the Pastor's Wife

YOU ARE ~~GOOD~~ ENOUGH

God created humanity in God's own image, in the divine image God created them, male and female God created them...God saw everything he had made: it was supremely good.

Genesis 1: 27, 31 (CEB)

One of the issues I have struggled with over the years is a feeling of inadequacy. Whenever I apply for a new job, begin a new endeavor, or seek out a new opportunity, the soundtrack of my mind is not encouraging. Every past failure I've experienced immediately jumps to the forefront, followed closely by all my fears of perceived future failure.

Instead of focusing on my strengths, I obsess over my weaknesses. Instead of looking at the ways God has prepared me for the task, I think of all the reasons he should choose someone else. The list is quite extensive:

- You're not talented enough
- You're not thin enough
- You're not trendy enough

Confessions of the Pastor's Wife

- You're not experienced enough
- You don't have the right credentials
- You don't have the right wardrobe

In talking with other women over the years, I find that I am not alone in my self-doubt. Most of us feel inadequate in some area of our lives. Part of the problem is that as women, we often compare ourselves to others. Instead of focusing on our own unique talents and gifts, we look at the gifts and talents of others and bemoan the attributes we lack.

The truth is, we were created for so much more than that! As women (and men), we were created in God's OWN image! God has put his likeness in us so that he might shine through us to others. As children of God, we are created in his grace, righteousness, love, and mercy, and at the end of that creative process, God proclaims that his creation is *supremely* good.

And part of that *supremely* good creation, my friend, is you. God doesn't look at you and see all of your faults and past mistakes. God doesn't wish you were prettier, thinner, more talented, or more credentialed. Instead, God looks at you and sees his beautiful creation. God looks at you and says, "You ARE enough for me because I created you. *You are mine.*"

Dear God, please help me to see that I am your creation. Let me be filled with your love and righteousness. Help me to let go of my past mistakes and failures so that I can see that in you, I am enough.

Confessions of the Pastor's Wife

Scripture Bytes

You are the one who created my innermost parts; you knit me together while I was still in my mother's womb. I give thanks to you that I was marvelously set apart. Psalm 139: 13-14 (CEB)

See what kind of love the Father has given to us in that we should be called God's children, for that is what we are! 1 John 3:1 (CEB)

Confessions of the Pastor's Wife

Confessions of the Pastor's Wife

WHY HIDING OUT IS NOT AN OPTION

It was still the first day of the week. That evening, while the disciples were behind closed doors because they were afraid of the Jewish authorities, Jesus came and stood among them. He said, "Peace be with you."... After eight days his disciples were again in a house and Thomas was with them. Even though the doors were locked, Jesus entered and stood among them. He said, "Peace be with you."

John 20: 19, 26 (CEB)

One of the most difficult aspects of being a United Methodist pastor's wife is having to find new employment each time we move. Over the past ten years, I have taught high-school English, a semester of third grade, been a substitute teacher, paraprofessional, done reading intervention, and performed freelance curriculum writing. Looking for employment is a scary, humbling process that always leaves me feeling a little battered and bruised.

When we moved to our first church appointment, the thought of looking for a job was overwhelming. "I'm never going to find a job!" I wailed to my husband as he was getting ready to leave for the church. He looked at me still lying in bed and replied, "No, not just laying around in your pajamas all day, you're not."

The truth is, I was hiding out. The fear of putting myself out there and facing rejection had me literally pulling the covers over my head. I think that fear is one of the enemy's greatest tools. Fear is paralyzing. Fear traps us and keeps us from stepping out in faith. Instead of trusting God to lead us down the path, we pitch a tent right in the middle of it and refuse to move.

When Jesus first came to the disciples after the Resurrection, they were trapped by fear. They had locked themselves in a room and had no plans to go anywhere anytime soon. Jesus' first words to his trembling disciples were, "Peace be with you!" One of the Greek definitions of this word translates to safety or security. Jesus was trying to tell his disciples that they were safe. They could open the doors and step into the light. And yet, one week after encountering the risen Christ, where do we find the disciples? Locked in a room—again!

I can't help but think Jesus was a little put out by their lack of faith. You see, Jesus had given them a job to do. They were supposed to be spreading the news of his Resurrection. But instead, they were trapped, imprisoned by their fear.

Once again, Jesus tells the disciples, "Peace be with you!" This time, however, he goes a bit further. Once Thomas had placed his hands in Jesus' wounds, Jesus said, "No more disbelief. Believe!" In other words, unlock the door and get to work.

The road for the disciples from the locked room to establishing the new church was not easy. They suffered, faced rejection, were humiliated, and sometimes failed. However, they were no longer bound by their fear. Instead, they called on the power of the

Confessions of the Pastor's Wife

Most High to guide them as they sought to spread his love and his grace. Although the work was hard, they were free from their incapacitating fear.

In those moments when we feel paralyzed with fear, it is important to remember that we serve a Lord who LIVES! And he has promised to walk down every dark and scary road we travel, bringing along his light to guide the way. However, we are responsible for taking that first step to freedom.

I don't know what you're hiding from today or what fear the enemy has placed in your heart that is keeping you trapped. Whatever it is, give it to God. Ask for his presence and his Spirit to help you unlock the doors and take those first steps to freedom. Remember Christ's words to his disciples, "No more disbelief. Believe!"

Dear God, help me to no longer be trapped by fear. Grant me your Spirit of Peace. Give me your strength to step out into the Light.

Scripture Bytes

Don't fear, because I am with you; don't be afraid, for I am your God. I will strengthen you; I will surely help you; I will hold you with my righteous strong hand.
Isaiah 41:10 (CEB)

...the peace of God that exceeds all understanding will keep your hearts and minds safe in Christ Jesus.
Philippians 4:7 (CEB)

Confessions of the Pastor's Wife

ACCEPTING CHANGE

Look! I am doing a new thing; now it sprouts up; don't you recognize it? I'm making a way in the desert, paths in the wilderness.

Isaiah 43:19 (CEB)

Not too long ago, I drove through the town where I was raised. Just for fun, I decided to check out my childhood home. It was remarkable how much it looked the same, from the cream-colored siding to the old aluminum screen door. I pulled up to the curb and imagined going inside. What would I see if I pulled open that squeaky aluminum door and stepped in? Would the little girl I once was still be contentedly coloring pictures on the golden carpet while the dings of pots and pans echoed from the kitchen? Would the living room still be full of dining room chairs covered in sheets and blankets as my sister and I hid out in our secret fort? Would my room still be painted a vivid pink, my bed adorned with the quilts my grandmothers and great-grandmothers had made?

The answer to all of these questions is, of course, a resounding no. If I walked into my childhood home, I would find hardwood floors, walls knocked out, new furniture, and strangers. My childhood has passed, and I have to confess that the reality of that makes me a little sad.

Confessions of the Pastor's Wife

I think that if we're honest, most of us can admit to finding change a challenge. How many times have you heard someone in church, school, work, Scouts, or sports say, "Well, we've always done it this way."? We get content with the status quo. Change can be uncomfortable, hurtful, and even sad at times. We don't want to say goodbye to our parents, send our children off to college, clean out our desk drawers, or close the door on our childhood.

And yet, change is a vital part of life. If change never happened, we would never grow. Think of the status quo like a flat line. In medical terms, a flat line is someone who lacks a pulse. Change is our pulse. It's a heartbeat that keeps us moving forward.

God is constantly working in our lives, changing and rearranging in order for us to grow closer to him. Often, we balk at those changes. *What do you mean you want me to quit my corporate job and go into ministry? Why should I spend my vacation money sponsoring a child I'll never meet? I don't want to go on a mission trip!*

Sometimes, changes in our lives occur that are painful and seem horribly unfair. We lose loved ones too soon, face powerful illnesses, endure unexpected financial hardships, or live through a catastrophic experience. The beauty of God's grace is that he can use even those changes for his good purposes.

When we embrace the changes life brings, both good and bad, then we are able to more fully live out the calling God has given us. Today, take a few moments to think about the changes you are facing or will soon be facing. Spend some time in prayer, giving those changes to God. Ask God for the spirit of wisdom to guide you in using those changes as a way to share God's love, grace, mercy, and peace with others.

Confessions of the Pastor's Wife

Dear God, thank you for continually moving in my life. Help me to see the changes I experience as growth opportunities. Grant me your spirit of wisdom to know how to use these changes to better serve you.

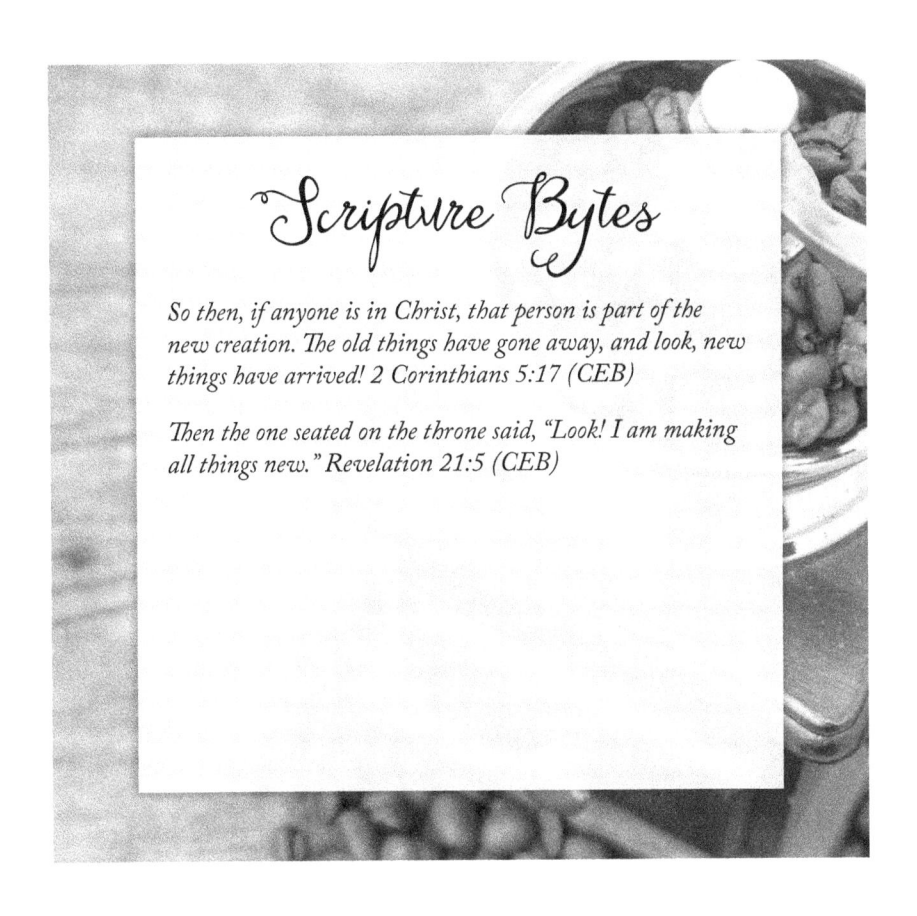

Scripture Bytes

So then, if anyone is in Christ, that person is part of the new creation. The old things have gone away, and look, new things have arrived! 2 Corinthians 5:17 (CEB)

Then the one seated on the throne said, "Look! I am making all things new." Revelation 21:5 (CEB)

Confessions of the Pastor's Wife

Confessions of the Pastor's Wife

I WILL REMEMBER

So I will always remind you of these things, even though you know them and are firmly established in the truth you know have. I think it is right to refresh your memory as long as I live in the tent of this body…and I will make every effort to see that after my departure you will always be able to remember these things.

2 Peter 1: 12-15 (NIV)

My grandmother is in the advanced stages of Alzheimer's disease. She doesn't remember what day it is or where she is. She doesn't recognize family members when they come to visit—even my dad, her youngest son, who comes and sits with her every day. My dad is a storyteller. In his mind live all of the stories of our family's past. When he sits with my grandmother, he tells her these stories. He tells her the stories she has locked away in her mind, recalling all of the people she has known and loved and created a lifetime full of memories with.

Over the past few years, I have been sharing these stories with my boys. They love these tales from the past because it reminds them of who they are and the people they come from. They know their great-grandpa was brave, so they can be brave too. They know their great grandparents valued family, so they will value family too. Even though most of these stories are about people they will never meet this side of eternity, the boys remember them, and their legacy lives on.

Confessions of the Pastor's Wife

This is what Peter was talking about when he told his readers that he would help them "remember these things." "These things" Peter refers to are the promises of God and the new life that all believers have through Jesus Christ. Peter, who had once denied Christ, dedicated his life to sharing the Gospel message so that all believers, both present and future, would remember who they are.

And who are we? We are the daughters and sons of the King. We are heirs to the throne of God! We have God's divine power living within us, giving us everything we need to navigate this life. We have God's glory and goodness, his great and precious promises. Through Christ, we have escaped the corruption in the world and live as a free people, redeemed by the blood of the Lamb.

Do you know who you are? Do you remember whose you are?

My grandmother remembers who she is every time she goes to Bible study and worship at the nursing home where she resides. As the hymns begin, their melodies wash over her and wipe away the disease that has devastated her mind. In that moment, music pours from her soul, and she remembers that she is the daughter of the King. She remembers God's promises in Scripture that were etched on her heart as a child. In those moments of worship, she is whole.

Do you remember who you are? Do you remember *whose* you are?

This week, take some time to remember who you are. Delve deep into the promises of God that are written in his Word. Etch them into your heart. Teach them to your children. Know that you are wholly and fully loved. Know that you are Redeemed. Remember that you are not bound by this world, but are free and most dearly loved.

Confessions of the Pastor's Wife

Do you need to remember who you are? Jesus said, "Remember me..."

Dear God, thank you that you have promised to always remember me. Thank you for redeeming me and setting me free. As I walk through this week, full of things unknown, help me to remember that I am your child and that you live within me.

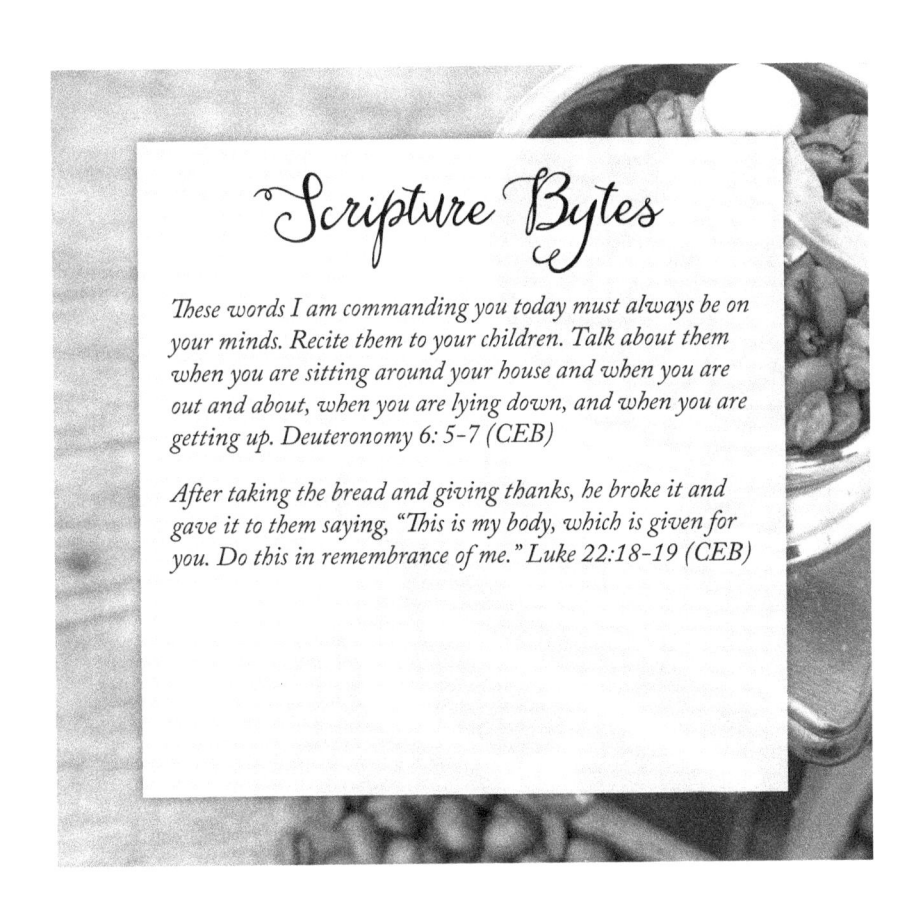

Scripture Bytes

These words I am commanding you today must always be on your minds. Recite them to your children. Talk about them when you are sitting around your house and when you are out and about, when you are lying down, and when you are getting up. Deuteronomy 6: 5-7 (CEB)

After taking the bread and giving thanks, he broke it and gave it to them saying, "This is my body, which is given for you. Do this in remembrance of me." Luke 22:18-19 (CEB)

Confessions of the Pastor's Wife

Confessions of the Pastor's Wife

STORMY DAYS

*The whole earth is filled with awe at your wonders;
where morning dawns, where evening fades,
you call forth songs of joy.*

Psalm 65:8 (NIV)

Recently, a morning dawned dark and stormy. I rose to greet the day with a mood to match the ominous clouds outside. All of my insecurities arose with me that morning, rolling across my mind like the thunder outside.

You've failed…you're going to fail…you won't be successful…don't try…don't strive…you're not good enough…give up your dreams, ambitions, and desires…don't reach for anything more…

And so I sat down…in the middle of my kitchen floor…on the little step stool I use when reading my Bible in the morning. Hugging my Bible to my chest, I poured out all of my tumultuous thoughts before God, big fat drops of doubt and fear splashing down before the One who knows a thought before it enters my mind.

"I can't do it," I said. "I'm not talented enough. I'm not cool enough. This women's ministry is never going to get off the ground. You can have my dreams back, each and every one, and I'll go be average and never dream about anything again."

Confessions of the Pastor's Wife

I lowered my Bible to my lap and opened it to where I had left off in the book of Acts the day before. Secretly, I was hoping for some divine promise to wend it's way like a lightning bolt straight from the page to my soul—some reassurance that all was going to be fine, that my fears and insecurities were unfounded and that God was going to take care of everything in a way that I could sum up in a thirty-second sound byte.

The truth is, God and I have never really had that kind of relationship. In my life, God often waits *through* the storm, letting the winds whirl and swirl around me—a quiet Presence standing still as the front passes by. God is okay with me getting a little windblown and wet. Perhaps he feels it builds faith.

After reading a bit, I stood up from the little step stool, pushing back the clouds that threatened to engulf me. I went through my morning routine, making lunches, getting the boys up and dressed, digging out a broken umbrella. And while the storm hadn't completely moved on, God's Presence was like my little broken umbrella. It kept me dry enough.

By the end of that gray and stormy day, the sun was shining in a cornflower blue sky. Huge, fluffy white clouds perched on the horizon. And I heard, once my own storm of doubt and insecurity had passed by, God speaking into the bright clear blue.

You know, whatever you pursue or don't pursue is your choice.

> *I gave you gifts and talents. It's up to you to decide what you do with them.*
>
> *But consider this: you and I communicate a lot through those gifts.*
>
> *Whether or not you choose to make a career of them doesn't matter to me.*

Confessions of the Pastor's Wife

What matters is that you do them, because it's how we talk.

And as long as we're talking, you're not a failure.

As long as we're talking, you're doing exactly what I designed you to do.

There are always going to be stormy days. It's a natural part of life. If we're willing, the storms can serve a tremendous purpose. Those storms, which the Enemy so hopes will destroy us, will actually make us stronger. Because even though it might feel like we're being buffeted along by the wind, God is there all the time. His love and his peace act as an umbrella over us, protecting us as the storm passes by.

I don't know what your personal storm is today. Maybe it's your marriage, your career, your children, or your health. Maybe you struggle with insecurity and doubt like me. Perhaps you've been waiting/longing/begging God to shout "Be STILL!" to the wind that howls all around you.

But, what if God is whispering, "Be still," to you? What if he's asking you to weather the storm? Or, an even scarier thought, to walk through it?

I think that the sun looks more radiant after a storm. The earth seems fresher somehow—cleansed and rejuvenated. The grass sparkles, there are rainbows on the pavement, and there are puddles to gleefully play in. There is promise, there is possibility, there is joy.

And we would never find any of it if we hadn't been through the storm.

Confessions of the Pastor's Wife

Dear God, thank you for walking with me through the storms of life. Help me to be still and listen for your voice, so that I might better follow you.

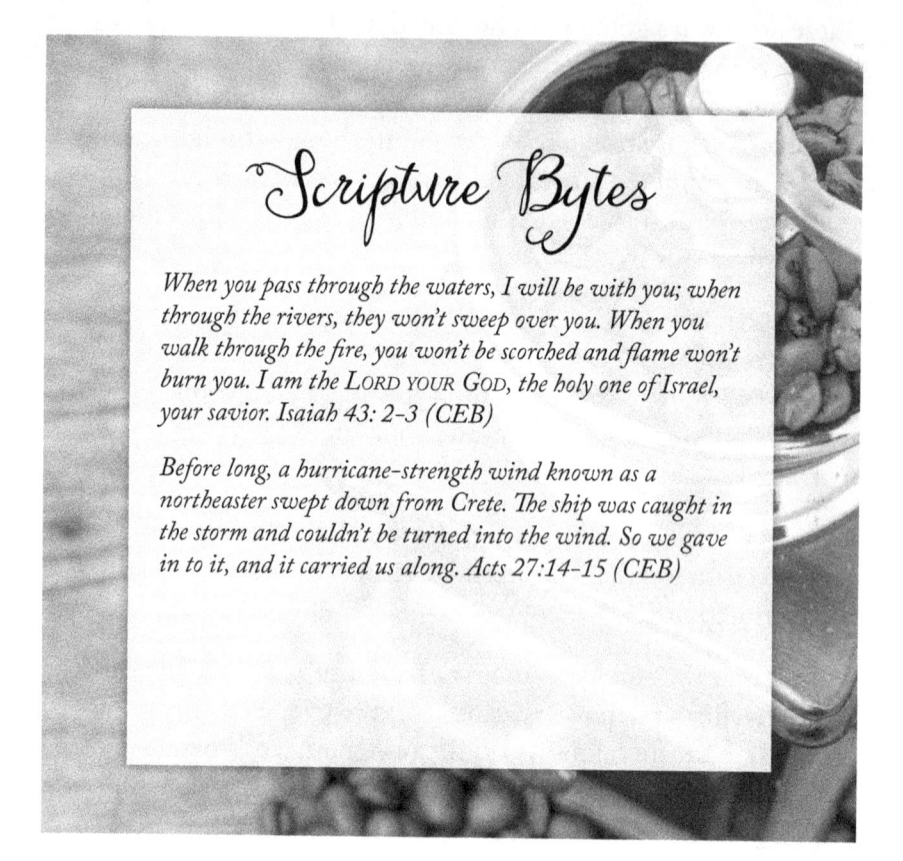

Scripture Bytes

When you pass through the waters, I will be with you; when through the rivers, they won't sweep over you. When you walk through the fire, you won't be scorched and flame won't burn you. I am the LORD YOUR GOD, the holy one of Israel, your savior. Isaiah 43: 2-3 (CEB)

Before long, a hurricane-strength wind known as a northeaster swept down from Crete. The ship was caught in the storm and couldn't be turned into the wind. So we gave in to it, and it carried us along. Acts 27:14-15 (CEB)

Confessions of the Pastor's Wife

SWIMMING INTO THE WAVES

The Lord is good and does the right thing; he teaches sinners which way they should go. God guides the weak to justice, teaching them his way. All the Lord's paths are loving and faithful for those who keep his covenant and laws. Please, for the sake of your good name, Lord, forgive my sins, which are many! Where are the ones who honor the Lord? God will teach them which path to take. They will live a good life, and their descendants will possess the land. The Lord counsels those who honor him; he makes his covenant known to them. My eyes are always looking to the Lord because he will free my feet from the net.

Psalm 25:8-15 (CEB)

Not too long ago, our family took a mini vacation to the lake. We rented a house right off the main channel of the lake. The house had a dock and, on our last evening, I decided to go for a swim and to watch the sunset from the water. After treading water for a few minutes and letting my body adjust to the current, I started to swim away from the dock. As it was evening, there were many boats heading back to shore for the night. The heavy boat traffic created a strong wake around the dock. Waves came rolling up, over and over. I could hear the dock creaking and groaning as it was rocked repeatedly—up and down and back and forth.

Confessions of the Pastor's Wife

At first I tried to push through the waves as I swam, using my arms to cut through the water and kicking my feet to make a path. As I paused for a moment to tread water and catch my breath, a wave moved underneath me and lifted me up. I allowed myself to be carried a little farther along my path. I suddenly realized that I could use the extra waves to my advantage and have a more productive swim.

Instead of channeling all of my body's energy into cutting through the waves, I decided to let go and allow the waves to do the heavy swimming for me, thereby reserving my energy for the swim back to the dock.

It occurred to me that many of us approach life trying to cut through the waves. We're constantly exerting energy trying to make something happen, prevent something from happening, or sustain something that is happening.

We say things like:

- I can fix my marriage, if I just try harder.
- I can get my child to be more motivated in school, if I just work with him more.
- I can lose this extra weight, if I just exercise more.
- I can make more money, if I just work harder.

We pull the burden of living onto our own shoulders instead of allowing God to carry us through. The result is that we only cry out to God for help when we feel our heads going under water.

The result of living a life pushing through waves is that we end up exhausted, burnt out, and sinking into the watery depths of our own failure.

Confessions of the Pastor's Wife

I think that God has a different strategy for our swim through life. God wants to be our strength. He wants to be that wave that carries us through the water. He's right there, waiting to take the burden from us. But so often, in our need to be in control, we don't let him. We fall into the trap of thinking, "I can do this on my own." We want to be independent, when from the beginning of creation, it is clear that we were designed to be co-dependent. We need God.

Best of all, God, the Creator of the universe, the Alpha and the Omega, the Redeemer and Sustainer, the One who IS, wants to help US! In fact, he has given us an abundance of resources to aid us, not the least of which is the Holy Spirit who dwells within us.

That's not to say that we don't have work to do. God's not sending some celestial cruise ship out for us to ride through this life. We're swimming—we have to keep moving to stay afloat! But God is there, pushing us through the water. He gives us strength, pulls us up when we can't go any further, renews us, and leads us on.

The Psalmist writes, "My eyes are always looking for the Lord…", and Jesus promised that when we seek, we SHALL find. So the next time you find yourself tempted to say, "I've got this; I can do it on my own," remember, you don't have to. God designed us to need him. Embrace that need and swim on, knowing that you have the power of the Lord to support you.

Dear God, thank you for pushing me through the waters of this life. Thank you for your strength, your power, and your presence. Help me to lean on you when things get rough. Help me to depend on you for my strength and hope.

Confessions of the Pastor's Wife

Scripture Bytes

Don't fear, because I am with you; don't be afraid, for I am your God. I will strengthen you, I will surely help you; I will hold you with my righteous strong hand. Isaiah 41:10 (CEB)

I ask that he will strengthen you in your inner selves from the riches of his glory through the Spirit. I ask that Christ will live in your hearts through faith. As a result of having strong roots in love, I ask that you'll have the power to grasp love's width and length, height and depth, together with all believers. I ask that you'll know the love of Christ that is beyond knowledge so that you will be filled entirely with the fullness of God. Ephesians 3:16-19 (CEB)

Confessions of the Pastor's Wife

WHEN YOU'RE JUST NOT FEELING THE FAITHFULNESS

Therefore, since we are surrounded by such a great cloud of witnesses, let us throw off everything that hinders and the sin that so easily entangles. And let us run with perseverance the race marked out for us, fixing our eyes on Jesus, the pioneer and perfecter of faith. For the joy set before him he endured the cross, scorning its shame, and sat down at the right hand of the throne of God. Consider him who endured such opposition from sinners, so that you will not grow weary and lose heart.

Hebrews 12:1-3 (NIV)

Twenty-four grams of carbs. A fifty-two on the Glycemic Index (which only goes up to 100). Bananas. No really, I'm talking about bananas. The bright yellow, half-moon shaped fruit that is rich and creamy and satisfying, especially with a tablespoon of peanut butter or Nutella. My favorite snack these past several weeks has betrayed my sense of food trust. As I stared at the numbers in bold black type, I wanted to cry out, "Curse you, bananas!"

Confessions of the Pastor's Wife

Two years ago, I worked hard to lose over fifty pounds. Over the past year, I've gained about ten of those pounds back. I can't blame it all on bananas. Sometimes, I just get tired of working to make healthy choices day in and day out. Sometimes, instead of passing on the cheesy potatoes, I just want to slam my hand down on the table and yell, "Pass the cheesy potatoes—NOW!" Sometimes, I want a break from conscious living. Sometimes, that attitude transfers over to my faith life as well.

There are times when living a life of faith wears me out. I don't want to do what God has on the agenda for today. I'm tired of "blooming where I'm planted," working hard to maintain a positive attitude, finding the God-moments in the midst of the everyday mess. Sometimes, instead of trying to see the other side of a situation, to empathize with those who are struggling, I just want to say, "You know what? Life is hard. Deal with it and move on."

Occasionally, when confronted with a negative, egotistical, or mean person, I would like to not model Christ-like behavior and instead simply say, "You're a real jerk and I don't like you."

Some days, my selfish, judgmental, hypocritical, uncaring nature kicks into overdrive, and I'd rather lay on the couch binging out on Hallmark movies and ice cream than doing the work God has placed before me.

But here's what I love, and I mean LOVE about the Lord, my God. His grace is infinitely big enough to cover up all of my absolute failures as a human being. In fact, when I fall off the healthy food bandwagon, God doesn't come to me and rub my nose into the extra pound or so flashing on the scale, ranting and raving like some overzealous personal trainer. Instead, he quietly whispers to my heart a message of grace and redemption.

Confessions of the Pastor's Wife

This is a lifelong journey, He says to me. *It's the culmination of healthy choices made over a lifetime that really counts. Don't beat yourself up. Just keep working toward our goal of living a healthy lifestyle.*

Likewise, when I feel fed up with living out the call to show God's love to those I meet on a daily basis, God doesn't typically give me the swift kick in the rear I deserve. Instead, God gives me a quiet place to rest my mind. He offers up time and space for me to focus on Him, to feel His presence, to renew and re-energize and refocus.

This is a lifelong journey, He says to me. *It's the culmination of choosing to follow the path that I've led you down over the course of your lifetime that really counts. Just keep looking to Me. Come to Me, talk to Me, rest in Me. Keep working toward our goal of living a life that reflects My Love and Grace. Just keep trying. I am with you, every step of the way.*

I am humbled by the grace and mercy our Creator has for me. I am convicted by his steadfast devotion. I am moved by his strength to get up and keep going. And I am hopeful, because of his perfect love, that I will one day hear him say, "Well done, good and faithful servant."

Dear God, thank you for not judging me. Thank you for knowing that we are on a lifelong journey. Thank you for understanding when I don't get it right. Thank you for encouraging me and renewing me in those moments when I just don't think I can go on. Guide me, please, Great Jehovah. Let your light and love shine through me.

Scripture Bytes

The Lord's cloud stayed over the dwelling during the day, with lightning in it at night, clearly visible to the whole household of Israel at every stage of their journey. Exodus 40:38 (CEB)

...even if our bodies are breaking down on the outside, the person that we are on the inside is being renewed every day. 2 Corinthians 4:16 (CEB)

Confessions of the Pastor's Wife

FORGET THE HUSTLE

Come to me, all you who are weary, and I will give you REST.

Matthew 11:28 (emphasis the author's) (NIV)

I was reading a book recently about how to fully live into your career goals. The author suggested in this book that one of the keys to achieving your dream job was to "hustle." Really? Hustle?

As a working mom, most of my days are pretty full. I get up in the mornings in "mom" mode, making lunches, getting children dressed, making coffee, arranging for some sort of semi-nutritional breakfast—you know the drill. Then I write for several hours during the day, pick the kids up from school, engage in family time, help my husband with dinner, bathe kids, read, and put kids to bed. Like most other women I know, I don't have any more hustle to give. Moreover, I don't know that I would give it if I had it.

One of the sad truths about American life is that we've manipulated the concept of hard work so that it has become an idol of busyness. We like the "hustle," regardless of how much we protest it. There's a certain adrenaline rush that comes from being busy. There's a high that comes from shoving thirty-six hours of activity into a twenty-four-hour day. We feel like we are conquerors in an epic battle for productivity.

We run from one scheduled activity to the next, max ourselves out on projects with tight deadlines, and sign up for any and every committee that's being offered. And we do this because, deep down, we think being busy gives our life meaning. The more we "hustle," the more we are achieving. And achieving, in our culture, means success.

However, God's design for our lives could not be more different. God doesn't want us to "hustle" through our lives. Rather, God says, "Come to me. Sit quietly in my presence. Find your rest in my peace. Be still. Know me. Listen. Wait."

In repentance and REST is your salvation; in quietness and trust is your strength. But you would have none of it.

Isaiah 30:15 (NIV) (author's emphasis)

When Jesus came to visit the house of Mary, Martha, and Lazarus, he didn't praise Martha for running around like a chicken with her head cut off, trying to make a perfect dinner for these unexpected guests. Rather, he praised her sister Mary, who did nothing but sit and listen to him speak.

God doesn't want us running around until our heads spin. We weren't made to hustle. Rather, God wants us still at his feet, listening to his Word, communing with him. God hardwired our brains for connection—connection with other human beings and connection with him. And when we get caught up in the "hustle," we miss those connections.

Don't get me wrong, we are supposed to be actively engaged in productive works, but those productive works stem from spending time resting in God's Presence. God has created us to do works—

Confessions of the Pastor's Wife

His works. We can't do the work God has placed before us if we're too tired and worn out from hustling all day long.

This week, take some time to rest in God. Sit quietly for a few moments reading his Word. Listen to some Christian music on the radio. Pray as you drive to work.

Return to your REST, my soul, for the Lord has been good to you.

Psalm 116:7 (author's emphasis) (NIV)

Dear God, help me to take time to rest in you this week. Renew my strength so that I may do your good works.

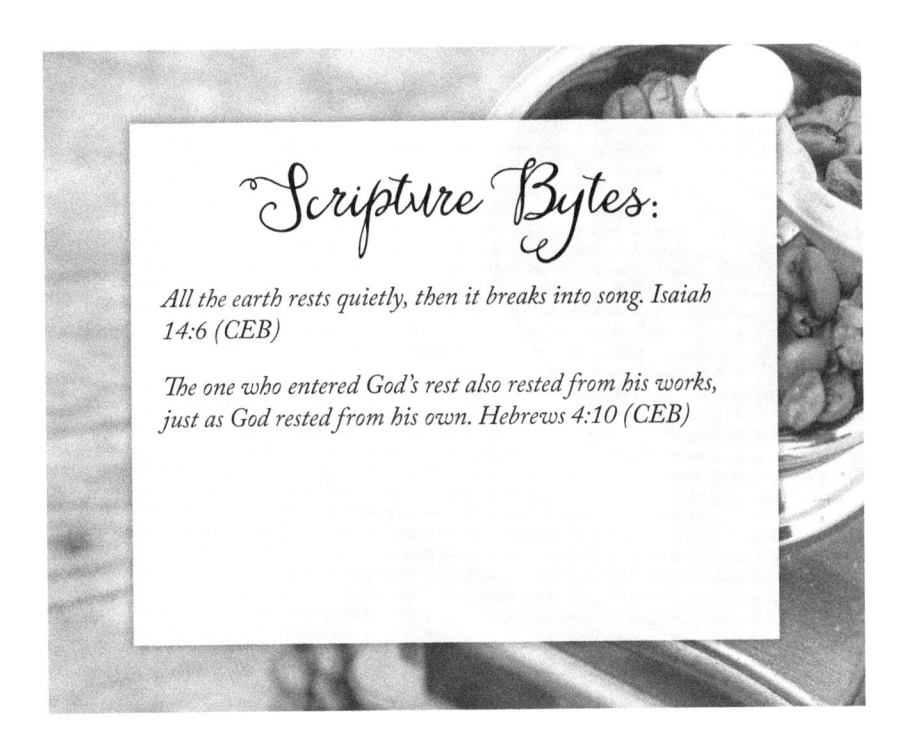

Scripture Bytes:

All the earth rests quietly, then it breaks into song. Isaiah 14:6 (CEB)

The one who entered God's rest also rested from his works, just as God rested from his own. Hebrews 4:10 (CEB)

Confessions of the Pastor's Wife

Confessions of the Pastor's Wife

LAY IT DOWN

This is how we know love: Jesus laid down his life for us, and we ought to lay down our lives for our brothers and sisters.

1 John 3:16 (CEB)

I must confess, I am a call screener. If I don't recognize a name and number, I don't pick up the phone. Often, even when I do recognize the name and number, I let the call go to voicemail. I just don't like to be disturbed. I could say that I only engage in this somewhat snooty practice when I'm working, but I don't like to be disturbed in general. It doesn't matter if I'm struggling to meet a tight deadline or watching *The Voice*, I don't want to be bothered.

My sister knows my avoidance of phone calls. If I don't answer my cell phone, she will call both the house and my husband to track me down. When I see her name pop up on the caller ID, I always answer with a disgruntled, "What?"

Like so many of us in our ego-centric culture, I get caught up in my "me bubble." I don't want to put down my work, turn off the T.V., or lay aside my book to focus on other people. And yet, as Jesus followers, that is precisely what we are called to do.

In 1 John, the apostle writes that Christians are known by their selfless love for others. As Jesus laid down his life for us, so we are to lay down our lives for others.

Confessions of the Pastor's Wife

- Laying down our lives for others is not always an act of martyrdom. Rather, I think that laying down our lives for others means popping our "me bubbles" and laying aside those things that keep us from engaging with and loving others. Laying aside our lives means laying aside those things that occupy the majority of our time, thoughts, and energy but that are not advancing the work of the Kingdom.

- Laying aside our lives might mean we need to spend less time at work and more time engaging with our families.

- Laying aside our lives might mean we need to close our computers, turn off our televisions, unplug our tablets, silence our cell phones and work on developing meaningful relationships with the people around us.

- Laying aside our lives might mean we actually introduce ourselves to our neighbors and invite them over for a barbeque instead of just waving as they drive by.

- Laying aside our lives might mean we skip a season of the kids' sports or activities, and volunteer as a family at a local food bank, homeless shelter, or animal rescue shelter.

- Laying aside our lives might mean we spend less money on coffee, shoes, clothes, or movies and donate more to a charitable organization.

- Laying aside our lives might mean sleeping less on Sunday mornings and participating more in worship with our fellow believers.

God calls us to actively engage in the world, to show his love by loving others. If Christ gave his life for us, can we not give more of our time, more of our money, more of our thoughts and energy and commitment, to sharing that love?

Confessions of the Pastor's Wife

This week, think about the things in your life you need to lay down. Ask God to reveal to you areas of your life that could be better dedicated to showing his love to others.

Dear God, show me the areas of my life that I need to lay down for you. Help me to be more aware of the needs of others, and to use my time, my talents, and my gifts to share your love with others.

Scripture Bytes

"Teacher, what is the greatest commandment in the Law?" He replied, "You must love the Lord your God with all your heart, with all your being, and with all your mind. This is the first and greatest commandment. And the second is like it: You must love your neighbor as you love yourself." Matthew 22:36-39 (CEB)

No one has greater love than to give up one's life for friends. John 15:13 (CEB)

Confessions of the Pastor's Wife

Confessions of the Pastor's Wife

BUILDING CONSISTENCY

People who live on milk are like babies who don't really know what is right. Solid food is for mature people who have been trained to know right from wrong. We must try to become mature and start thinking about more than just the basic things we were taught about Christ.

Hebrews 5:13-6:1 (CEB)

Sometimes I like experimenting with healthy foods. Over the past few months, I've been working on making waffles out of chocolate protein powder. While the flavor is pretty good, the consistency is a bit off. Waffles really aren't supposed to be crunchy.

As Jesus people, I think we often lack consistency in our faith walk. Most of us desire to grow in our faith, to become mature believers. However, we don't really engage in doing the things that will get us there. We don't make time to read Scripture, our prayers are interrupted by work or kids or burning dinner, we forgo weekly worship for sports or brunch or extra sleep. We aren't maturing in our faith because we're not consistently practicing it.

I know what you're going to say, "But I..."

Confessions of the Pastor's Wife

1. ...don't have time to read my Bible.
2. ...don't understand the Bible when I try to read it.
3. ...have to take my kids to sports activities.
4. ...only have Sunday mornings to spend with my family.
5. ...get really bored in worship.
6. ...don't feel God speaking to me.
7. ...get distracted when I try to pray.
8. ...don't know if God is really listening.

I get it, I truly do. I've said many of these same things myself. But here's the thing—we are called by the One who created us to actually *grow* in spiritual maturity. God doesn't want to be a babysitter. God wants to be in a mature relationship with his children! What an amazing honor that is! However, we can't have that relationship if we're not willing to consistently put in the work required to maintain it.

So, what do we need to do in order to become mature Jesus people? My friends, we need consistency. Here are a few tips to build consistency in our faith walk.

1. Read the Bible.

Find a translation that speaks to you (i.e., one that you understand). Go to Bible Gateway and read through various translations to see which one you like. Set aside an extra ten minutes in your day to read some Scripture. Write verses down that speak to you and post them around your house, office, or car. Start small. Read through the book of Philippians, Ruth, or 1

John. And pray. God's Spirit reveals the Scriptures to us, so ask God for that Spirit while you read.

2. Pray often.

Prayer is a conversation. It doesn't have to be fancy or poetic. Just talk to God. Thank God for the day, for the coffee, for the warm clothes fresh from the dryer. Thank God for the work you have to do, even if it's annoying. Tell God what you're thinking about. He knows, but he also likes to hear it from you. What are you struggling with? What are you worried about? Who are you worried about? Just talk…in the car, while pouring your coffee, while standing at the copy machine, waiting in line, or tossing clothes in the wash. Just talk…

3. Engage in worship.

Go to church. Worship with fellow believers. Maybe you don't like the music or the sermon or the liturgy…who cares? If you ask God to meet you in worship, he'll show up. Ask God to be there, regardless of the songs that are sung or the message that is delivered. Focus on God. Listen to the words of the hymns. Take time to pray. Pay attention to the message. Praise God for all he has done. And, ask for his presence to speak to you as you worship.

"Let's grow up, if God is willing," the author of Hebrews writes. I think God is willing…we just need to practice consistency.

Dear God, help me to be more consistent in my faith. Open up time in my day to spend with you. Guide my reading of your word, my conversations with you, and my worship of you.

Confessions of the Pastor's Wife

Scripture Bytes

God's goal for us is to become mature adults—to be fully grown, measured by the standard of the fullness of Christ. Ephesians 4:13 (CEB)

Therefore, get rid of all ill will and all deceit, pretense, envy, and slander. Instead, like a newborn baby, desire the pure milk of the word. Nourished by it, you will grow into salvation, since you have tasted that the Lord is good. 1 Peter 2:1-3 (CEB)

Confessions of the Pastor's Wife

IMPERFECT PERFECTION

He said to me, "My grace is enough for you, because power is made perfect in weakness." So I'll gladly spend my time bragging about my weaknesses so that Christ's power can rest on me.

2 Corinthians 12:9 (CEB)

As a writer, I hate writing. It's hard. There are days when I fight for every word that is written on the page. Often, when I'm finished, I feel like it's just not good enough. The problem is that I'm striving for perfection. I want my work to be the absolute best—not the best that it can be or the best that I can do—the *best*, period. I have this innate need to succeed and to please in the process of succeeding. This is a dangerous combination.

The truth is, if we base our success on how others perceive us, we're never going to get it right. We will always strive, but never achieve, because we were not made to be perfect. The end result of striving for perfection is exhaustion, depression, and an attitude of defeat.

Let me give you another example. Our house is almost always a disaster. We have two little boys and two dogs who have free rein in the house. My husband and I both work. On any given day, there are toys, blankets, and discarded pajamas strewn

Confessions of the Pastor's Wife

throughout the living room, dining room, and bedrooms. Dog food is scattered about the kitchen floor. Dishes are piled in the sink, the counters are covered in mail, and the dining room table is a hodgepodge of books, games, art supplies, cups, electronic devices, papers, and napkins. I haven't even begun on the piles of clothes in the bedrooms or four baskets of laundry that need to be folded.

When I walk into friends' homes and see how well put together they are, my insides start to squirm. *How do they do it?* I think. *What's wrong with me? Why am I such a terrible housekeeper? I just don't measure up…*

My house will never be perfect…well maybe, after my boys leave the nest! For now, I could spend my entire day cleaning, only to have it wrecked by the following afternoon. We live in our home and it looks like it.

Similarly, our lives can be a great big mess. We live them and it looks like it. We make mistakes. We say hurtful things. We ignore situations we should attend to. We don't give enough to those in need. We get mad at our spouses and our children. We don't think things through enough. We overextend ourselves. We're human. And, as a wonderful project editor once reminded me, as long as humans are responsible for the work that is being done, it's never going to be perfect.

Fortunately for us, God has zero expectations for perfection. In fact, God wants us to embrace our imperfections, because our imperfections allow his perfection to shine through.

I have often found that the writing I deem to be the "worst" is actually what speaks to people the most. I think it's because when I'm feeling the least confident about a piece of writing, I give more of it to God. And when God steps in to guide the work, it

Confessions of the Pastor's Wife

is infinitely better than what I could accomplish on my own. And so, I'm trying to embrace the imperfections, both of my work and in my life.

This week, take a few moments to think about those areas in your life where you are striving for perfection. What are you trying to accomplish? Who are you trying to please? What would happen if you gave that area of your life to God? Can you allow God to redefine your idea of success?

You are imperfectly perfect, which is all that God desires you to be.

Dear God, thank you for letting me be imperfectly perfect. Help me let go of my need for perfection and my need to please that I may better serve you.

Confessions of the Pastor's Wife

Scripture Bytes

Now really, who is divine except the Lord? And who is a rock but our God? Only God! The God who equips me with strength and makes my way perfect, who makes my step as sure as the deer's, who lets me stand securely on the heights…
Psalm 18:31-33 (CEB)

God is indeed my salvation; I will trust and won't be afraid. Yah, the Lord, is my strength and my shield; he has become my salvation." Isaiah 12:2 (CEB)

Confessions of the Pastor's Wife

WHEN LIFE FEELS LIKE A ROLLER COASTER

"Come to me, all of you who are struggling hard and carrying heavy loads, and I will give you rest. Put on my yoke, and learn from me. I'm gentle and humble. And you will find rest for yourselves."

Matthew 11:28-29 (CEB)

A couple of years ago, my husband and I decided to explore the Harry Potter world at Universal Studios in Orlando. We got there early in the morning to avoid long lines. As we had left the kids behind at Disney with family, we decided to hit all three of the roller coasters right in a row. About midway through the third coaster, as my head was being banged from side to side and my stomach was lurching up and down, I really wanted to get off the ride! When it was over, I stumbled from the car, looked at my husband and said, "I need to sit down!" Forty-five minutes and one Butterbeer later, I finally felt more like myself again. But I was definitely done with roller coasters for the rest of the day.

Sometimes, life can be a roller coaster of sorts. I don't know about you, but my mind can swing around and around trying to

Confessions of the Pastor's Wife

engage, create and problem-solve from several different areas at once. There's marriage, kids, work, dinner and ministry to focus on. Often, managing all of it can leave me feeling both dizzy and disoriented. I find that I'm ready to jump off the ride, but unfortunately, I'm still in the middle of it!

In those times when I feel like I need a brain massage, I sit down on the little step-stool in the kitchen that is my Bible study spot and bow my head over my Bible. I work hard to clear my mind and to focus on the image of the Holy Spirit wrapping himself around me like a snug blanket.

As I float for a few minutes, pushing aside all thoughts of people and situations I need to pray over, I hear God asking me, "What do you need?" And the answer that comes is, *rest*.

The above verses from the book of Matthew float through my conscious mind like wisps of campfire smoke coming up from the Spirit's flame in my heart. *Come to me. I will give you rest.*

The context of this passage is the burden that the religious leaders were placing on the people. The religious leaders were demanding more than the people could ever possibly give—making all sorts of rules and regulations no human could ever follow completely. Jesus was attempting to simplify things. He implored the people not to get caught up in the human rules and regulations of the church and worship. Rather, he said, follow my lead. Love God. Love others.

Jesus is talking about a spiritual rest. That is something we don't do very well in our noisy, always engaged, frenetic society. We want to go, to move, to do, to achieve, until our lives begin to look like a grocery store checklist instead of the beautiful tapestry they were designed to be. That's not to say we won't be burdened. Living is HARD WORK. A tapestry doesn't come together with a few simple stitches. But through it all, we have the gift of God's presence, God's love, and God's grace. It's hard to see those things, however, when we don't take time to find rest for our souls.

What is the roller coaster life has put you on right now? What is making you feel dizzy, disoriented, and overwhelmed? Whatever it is, you are not alone. We're all on this crazy behemoth together. And while your brain might hurt from trying to problem-solve, or your heart might ache from grief and pain, or your stomach might be doing flip-flops from anxiety and fear, know that God is right there with you. Know that God longs to give your soul rest. Know that He is right there beside you on this roller-coaster holding your hand. So hang on. Think about your tapestry. God is not interested in checking things off of our life lists. He's interested in creating a work of art.

Dear God, help me find my rest in you.

Confessions of the Pastor's Wife

Scripture Bytes

Come to me, all you who are weary and burdened, , and I will give you rest. Take my yoke upon you, and learn from me, for I am gentle and humble in heart, and you will find rest for your souls. Matthew 11:28-29 (NIV)

Come to Me, all you who labor and are heavy-laden and overburdened, and I will cause you to rest. [I will ease and relieve and refresh your souls.] Take My yoke upon you and learn of Me, for I am gentle (meek) and humble (lowly) in heart, and you will find rest (relief and ease and refreshment and recreation and blessed quiet) for your souls. Matthew 11:28-29 (Amplified Bible)

Are you tired? Worn out? Burned out on religion? Come to me. Get away with me and you'll recover your life. I'll show you how to take a real rest. Walk with me and work with me—watch how I do it. Learn the unforced rhythms of grace. I won't lay anything heavy or ill-fitting on you. Keep company with me and you'll learn to live freely and lightly. Matthew 11:28-29 (Message Bible)

Confessions of the Pastor's Wife

EMBRACING YOUR GIFTS

There are different kinds of gifts, but the same Spirit distributes them. There are different kinds of service, but the same Lord. There are different kinds of working, but in all of them and in everyone it is the same God at work. Now to each one the manifestation of the Spirit is given for the common good.

1 Corinthians 12:4-7 (NIV)

Cher hair. That's how we in my family lovingly refer to my eighth-grade perm fiasco. Cher hair. I didn't intend to emulate Cher's wildly coiffed late '80s 'do. I just wanted curls—the cute spiral kind that gently rolled across your shoulders like tiny miniature Slinkys that all of the teen models were sporting in my copies of Teen magazine. Unbeknownst to my hairdresser (who truly meant well), my hair tends to have a lot of natural body. Not curl—there are no curls. Just poof, which my hairdresser must have missed in her initial assessment of my hair because, as my hair is also very thick, she decided it would need a double perm in order for the curls to stick. If you've ever wondered what the outcome of a double perm on naturally poofy hair equals, I can tell you—Cher hair.

Needless to say, I made quite the entrance at school the following day. My eighth-grade history teacher told my dad that I looked very dramatic, like a movie star. Most everyone else in our small Bible-belt town just thought I looked silly. And really, they were right. It was ridiculous. But, of course, at that point I was stuck with it. I learned to make do with my crazy 'do. I turned bandanas into head bands and tried to keep the wild mass of curls away from my face. And my family has lots of photographic ammunition for public humiliation if they ever so desire.

The lesson I learned that year was that my hair was not made to perm. No amount of chemical combinations will ever take my thick, poofy hair and transform it into strands of beautifully woven spirals. It's just not going to happen—ever. I eventually found a hairdresser who introduced me to the concept of hair straighteners. It was a life-changing moment, because while my hair was not created to be curled, it was absolutely made to be straightened.

There's a process of self-embracing I think we all have to go through in life. So often, we long to be different from who God created us to be. We pass over all of the wonderful and unique aspects of our created being and focus on those things we find to be lacking. Instead of playing to our strengths, we constantly worry over and bemoan our weaknesses. "I need to be more _____," we think, instead of saying, "I can really use _____ to make a difference in the world!"

God promises us that he has endowed each and every one of his children with specific gifts and abilities. *Specific gifts AND abilities.* And he has given us these traits and talents to be used for HIS glory. God created us to be who HE wants us to be! God doesn't look at us and say, "Man, I wish I had given this one more organizational skills!" Instead, he sees a beautiful child whom he created to reflect his glory and to bring his kingdom on earth.

Confessions of the Pastor's Wife

So, instead of focusing on the things you wish you were, try looking instead at who you are. See yourself as a child of God first, and then work to discover (or rediscover) all of the gifts and abilities God has placed within you. Use those abilities to do something positive. Show God's love in a real and meaningful way through being who you are—not who you think you should be.

This week, take a quick assessment of your gifts and abilities. In the space provided, write down three things you are good at. Don't judge them, just write them. Maybe you're an expert at baking. Perhaps you can starch a shirt like no one else. Are you a master gardener? Are you skilled at teaching, leading, or encouraging? Do you have a head for numbers, logic, and organization? Whatever it is, write it down below.

Three Things I Do Well

1. _____
2. _____
3. _____

Now that you have established some gifts and abilities God has blessed you with, think about three ways you might use these gifts in God's service. Can you arrange a pot of flowers to brighten someone's day? Can you help a single mother figure out a budget that works for her and her family? Can you make a home-cooked meal for someone in need? Write them below, then make a plan this week to carry out those acts of service, praising God for the opportunity to use your gifts in such a way.

Confessions of the Pastor's Wife

Three Ways I Can Use These Gifts for God's Service

1. _____
2. _____
3. _____

Dear God, thank you for entrusting me with these gifts and abilities. Help me as I seek to use them in your service. Let them bring glory and honor to you.

Scripture Bytes

We have different gifts that are consistent with God's grace that has been given to us. Romans 12:6 (CEB)

And serve each other according to the gift each person has received, as good managers of God's diverse gifts. 1 Peter 4:10 (CEB)

Confessions of the Pastor's Wife

WHEN THE FUTURE IS SCARY AND UNCERTAIN

Then Job replied to the Lord: "I know that you can do all things; no purpose of yours can be thwarted. You asked, 'Who is this that obscures my plans without knowledge?' Surely I spoke of things I did not understand, things too wonderful for me to know."

Job 42:1-3 (NIV)

When I was a girl, I had my entire future mapped out. It stretched in front of me like a golden yellow-brick road, easy to follow and clear to see. As I got older, the future became less clear. The golden bricks turned a dull brassy color. Trees grew up in the path. Sharp turns blocked my view. I was less confident, less hopeful. Sometimes, I was downright scared.

There are times in our lives when the future can look pretty tough. When my niece was three years old, she needed heart surgery. A blood vessel that was supposed to disappear before birth had grown around her trachea and needed to be removed. However, because of the placement of the vessel, the surgery was complicated and the recovery fairly painful. Needless to say, we were all a little stressed!

Confessions of the Pastor's Wife

My dad stopped sleeping. My mom stopped eating. My sister started maniacally planning. My brother-in-law was maniacally working. And I was in a constant state of denial, thinking that surely, at the last moment, the radiologist who first found the vessel would come bursting into the operating room shouting, "Oops! My bad!! You don't need to do this after all!" The whole situation was terrifying, all the more so because we had no control over any of it.

When future events are looming and you have no control over them, it can become very easy to fall into the gaping hole that is fear. Fear is one of the enemy's most powerful and destructive tools. Fear immobilizes us. Fear keeps us from moving forward. Fear causes us to back away from a problem rather than facing it head-on. Fear moves us into the darkness of doubt and despair.

That hole of fear is a useless empty place where nothing good can be accomplished. That hole takes us farther away from the peace and assurance that God has promised each of his children.

"And lo, I will be with you always..." Jesus told his disciples. "Even unto the ends of the earth." The ends of the earth for us during this time of uncertainty included the operating table, a place where God could go even when we, the family, could not. God could go with our little girl into the operating room. God could be with her through the surgery. God could, and did, go with her into the recovery room. And God was with her as she awoke and experienced pain like she had never felt before.

God is there in the midst of our scary, tough uncertain futures. He's already making a way for us that we cannot even see! And no matter what happens, He's going to be there—even if it all goes awry.

Confessions of the Pastor's Wife

When Job was in the midst of his suffering, God came to him, not to offer words of comfort, but to remind him that he (God) was the Creator and Sustainer of all things. It was God who was there at the beginning of time, God who created all things in Heaven and Earth, God who sets out the course of life, and God who has ultimate wisdom and understanding.

"Who of you by worrying can add a single hour to your life?" Jesus asked his disciples. The answer? No one.

I don't know what the future holds for any of us. Some of it will be scary, some of it will hurt. But some of it will be wonderful and beautiful as well. And through it all, God will be there, our Strength and our Song to the end.

Dear God, thank you for promising to be with us, no matter what. Help me to look to the future with strength and hope, not with uncertainty and fear. Whatever may happen on the road ahead, help me to feel your Presence and your Peace. May your Spirit be a guiding light unto my path.

Scripture Bytes

I'm convinced that nothing can separate us from God's love in Christ Jesus our Lord: not death or life, not angels or rulers, not present things or future things, not powers, or height, or depth, or any other thing that is created. Romans 8:37-39 (CEB)

Before the mountains were born, before you birthed the earth and the inhabited world—from forever in the past to forever in the future, you are God. Psalm 90:2 (CEB)

Confessions of the Pastor's Wife

GOD IS NOT A GPS

"The God who made the world and everything in it is the Lord of heaven and earth and does not live in temples built by human hands. And he is not served by human hands, as if he needed anything. Rather, he himself gives everyone life and breath and everything else. From one man he made all the nations, that they should inhabit the whole earth; and he marked out their appointed times in history and the boundaries of their lands. God did this so that they would seek him and perhaps reach out for him and find him, though he is not far from any one of us. 'For in him we live and move and have our being.'"

Acts 17:24-28 (NIV)

I must confess, I tend to be directionally challenged. It's a family trait, handed down through many generations. On a recent trip to Omaha, my sister and I needed both Greta (my in-vehicle GPS) and Google to navigate the city. Even with these two "expert" guides, we still managed to drive by one of our destinations three times. Apparently NASA technology can only get you so far!

I sometimes feel directionally challenged in life too. The eighteen-year-old me would be utterly flabbergasted by the road map the thirty-eight-year-old me has managed to create these past twenty years. And to tell you the truth, I still have no idea where we're going. A few summers ago, I seriously considered

Confessions of the Pastor's Wife

making a significant career change. It would have been a true leap of faith and I was right on the cusp of jumping. I spent hours agonizing over the decision, weighing the pros and cons, talking with friends and family, praying over and over for a sign.

"I need some direction!" was my constant cry to God. And then came these words from a woman much wiser than me: "Maybe there is no right answer...."

It hit me in that moment, as I read her words of truth, that I had been using God much like I use my GPS. I was trying to plug in a destination and retrieve specific directions. But God is not always interested in specific directions. If he were, the Israelites would have arrived in Cana within four weeks, not forty years! God doesn't want to be our GPS system, telling us to go straight, turn left, make a u-turn, head south. Rather, God wants to be in a relationship with the children he created.

God had a purpose for walking the Israelites around the desert for forty years. They had spent hundreds of years away from him, following the customs and beliefs of another people. The Israelites were not ready for the "promised land." They needed time to come to know God once more, and to understand who they were in him. They needed those forty years to become the people of God.

That doesn't mean that God won't give us directions. Directions are important. I still call my parents and ask for advice. However, the guidance and direction we receive is the byproduct of an authentic and intimate relationship with God.

When we spend time with God, whether it be in prayer, worship, Scripture, meditation, etc., we invite God to dwell within us. The Holy Spirit spreads throughout our being, like a fine mist sweeping up and settling in over a field. God permeates us, enfolds us, fills us up so that, as Paul writes, we "live and

Confessions of the Pastor's Wife

move and breathe in Him." In God we find ourselves and that knowledge shapes where we go and what we do.

The road maps of our lives are never going to be straight and clear. There will be unexpected road closures, detours, breakdowns, and pit stops. And sometimes, the directions won't be very clear. But I think that if we live a life built around a relationship with our Creator, we'll always be headed in the right direction.

Dear God, help me to get lost in you, so that I may find my way back home.

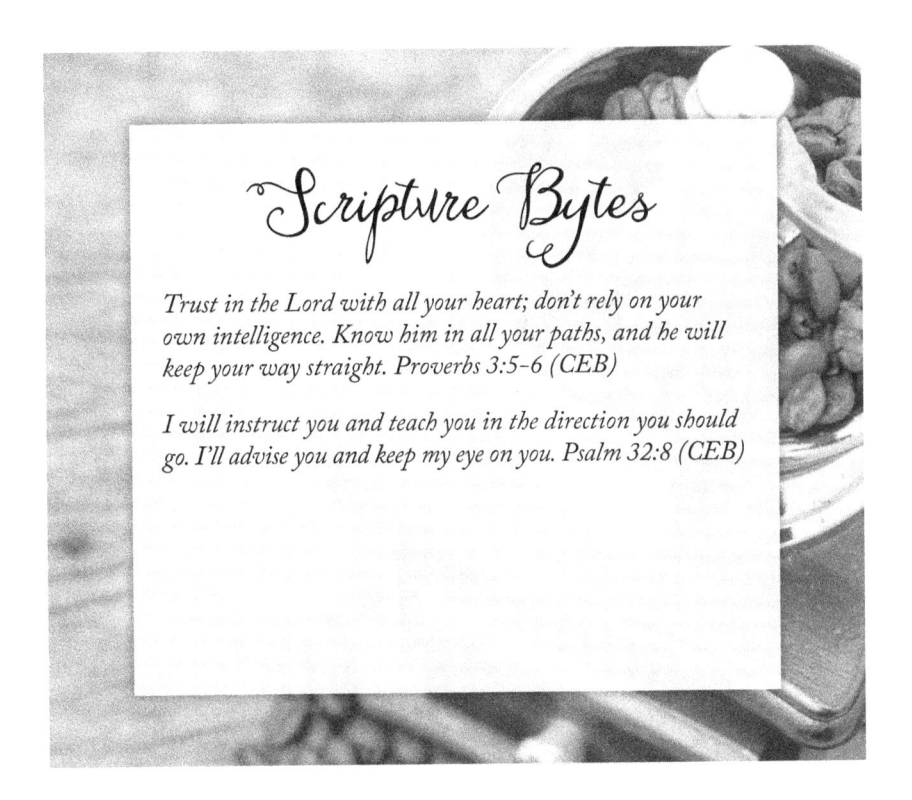

Scripture Bytes

Trust in the Lord with all your heart; don't rely on your own intelligence. Know him in all your paths, and he will keep your way straight. Proverbs 3:5-6 (CEB)

I will instruct you and teach you in the direction you should go. I'll advise you and keep my eye on you. Psalm 32:8 (CEB)

Confessions of the Pastor's Wife

Confessions of the Pastor's Wife

CALLA LILLY GRACE

The grace of our Lord was poured out on me abundantly, along with the faith and love that are in Christ Jesus.

1 Timothy 1:14 (NIV)

"The calla lilies are back!" I call through the screen door, squatting down in front of our little garden. I smile at the tiny green shoot pushing its way through, up out of the dark earth.

The calla lilies came up in late spring, slowly and nonchalantly stepping into the warmth of May. These flowers have been our pale, soft, plum sentinels of summer. I love them. For me, these calla lilies have become a symbol of God's magnificent grace.

My husband and I planted three pots of calla lilies a couple of years ago. It was an impulse buy. I had no idea whether or not they were native to Missouri, would thrive in our mostly sun-filled environment, or if I would remember to go out and water them regularly. They were pretty, they were on sale, and I wanted them.

They did okay that first summer. The leaves grew and we had one pretty fluted lily pop up by fall. I left them in the ground over the winter, not knowing there was anything else to do with plants, and didn't give them much thought until someone pointed out that calla lily bulbs are supposed to be brought indoors for the winter.

Imagine my surprise, then, when my husband came in one day after work the next spring and said, "You've got a lily coming up". Indeed, I did—an astoundingly deep, rich, plum lily had fluted forth from the ground with no help at all from me. I marveled at its beauty. I'd never seen anything like it.

But then came the drought. Everything dried up, including my beautiful lily. Our grass turned brown, weeds took over the garden, and I left it, not expecting anymore life to come forth from the dry, wasted dirt.

And so again, I was surprised when, late the following spring, THREE lilies opened themselves to our garden once more. They weren't the rich deep plum of the previous summer, but a softer, paler pink sister. They were also taller and stronger than any of the lilies had been before. In the middle of the hot and humid August sun, those lovely ladies still stood tall.

These lilies are a tangible reminder to me of God's grace. Even when we feel we're done, God's grace comes pouring in, giving us new life, new meaning, new purpose, and new strength. God renews us over and over again. More than that, God's grace transforms us. We become a new creation. And, like my lilies, God makes us stronger and more plentiful in each passing season. When we feel like the ground beneath our feet is hard, dry, and barren, God's grace comes breaking through our desert land to renew and replenish us.

Perhaps you are facing a season of drought. Maybe you feel stuck in a job you hate. Maybe a relationship has gone stale. Maybe your finances seem to be drying up. Maybe you are experiencing loss and grief, feeling lost and lonely in the midst of your despair.

Confessions of the Pastor's Wife

Whatever desert place you find yourself in today, remember, God's grace is there. Call on the One who is able to renew your strength. Ask your Sustainer to pour his Spirit over the parched earth of your life and to bring renewal.

The calla lilies are in bloom again. And as I watch them, I realize—so am I.

Dear God, let your grace rain down over my parched soul. Let me see it blooming in my life. Quench my thirst, and renew my spirit.

Scripture Bytes

Let God grant us grace and bless us; let God make his face shine on us, so that your way becomes known on earth, so that your salvation becomes known among all the nations.
Psalm 67:2 (CEB)

From his fullness, we have all received grace upon grace.
John 1:16 (CEB)

Confessions of the Pastor's Wife

Confessions of the Pastor's Wife

WAIT AND SEE

We continually ask God to fill you with the knowledge of his will through all the wisdom and understanding that the Spirit gives, so that you may live a life worthy of the Lord and please him in every way: bearing fruit in every good work, growing in the knowledge of God, being strengthened with all power according to his glorious might so that you may have great endurance and patience, and giving joyful thanks to the Father, who has qualified you to share in the inheritance of his holy people in the kingdom of light.

Colossians 1:9-12 (NIV)

I tend to be rather impulsive. I like spur of the moment road trips across several states. If something catches my eye in a store, I like being able to buy it then and there. When I get an idea for a ministry project, I tend to just dive right in before swimming through the details. Impulsivity is something I am comfortable with.

My husband is the exact opposite. He never builds/starts/buys anything without thorough research and planning. If I'm perfectly honest, it drives me absolutely crazy, especially when it involves multiple trips to three different home improvement stores. By the time I'm ready to scream, "Just pick something already!" we're moving onto store number two.

Confessions of the Pastor's Wife

But, if I'm still being perfectly honest, his methodical nature is a quality that I love and cherish. His detailed planning of everything allows me to rest assured in all of the decisions he makes. I trust him and I value his opinion because I know it's carefully formulated with lots of consumer research. While I'm diving into the deep water, he's standing above, holding a life preserver!

God is not impulsive either. As it took almost 800 years from the promise made to Abraham about inheriting the land of Canaan and the actual inheritance of said land, I would say that God is the direct opposite of impulsive! God is a methodical planner.

And yet, even though I know that God is not impulsive, even though I know that he has a plan and has painstakingly attended (and is attending to) every detail, I still find myself screaming, "Just do something already! I'm tired of waiting!"

Sometimes, I even try and push God to force his hand. Instead of waiting and trusting in God's omnipotence and sovereignty over my life, I jump in and try to get the ball rolling myself. I pull the, "Well, if you're not going to do anything about it, then I guess I'll have to" card. Needless to say, it never works. In fact, quite the opposite really. My refusal to let go of situations and trust in God most often moves me farther back than I was to begin with. I create situations in which God has to act, but it's not to move my life forward; rather, it's to clean up the new mess I've made.

The truth is, God doesn't need us to do his job for him. As the Creator and Sustainer of the Universe, he's got it pretty well under control. Moreover, he has a plan that he has been in the process of implementing since the dawn of time. And God has graciously and perfectly placed us within that plan. While my impulsivity doesn't take me out of God's perfect plan (for nothing

Confessions of the Pastor's Wife

in heaven or earth or below can keep us from the great love of God), it can make the road a bit more difficult.

And so, I wait, begrudgingly at times, but with the knowledge that he who knit me together in my mother's womb is putting it all together.

Dear God, thank you for being a methodical planner. Help me to patiently wait for you, using the time to draw closer to you.

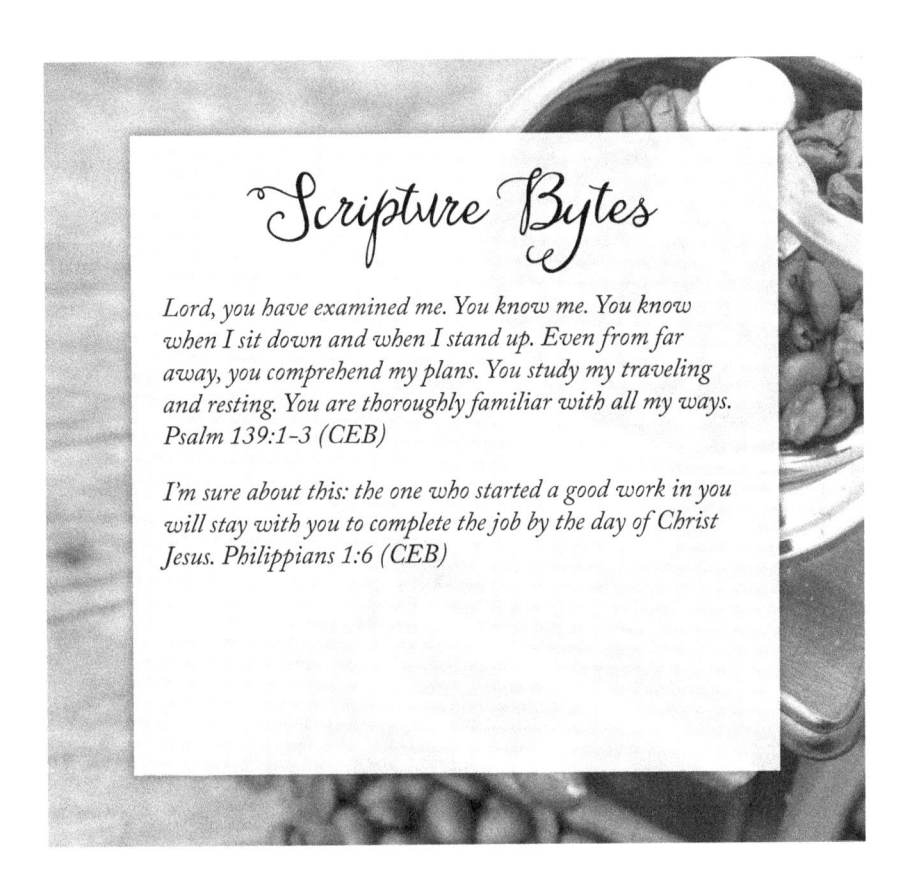

Scripture Bytes

Lord, you have examined me. You know me. You know when I sit down and when I stand up. Even from far away, you comprehend my plans. You study my traveling and resting. You are thoroughly familiar with all my ways. Psalm 139:1-3 (CEB)

I'm sure about this: the one who started a good work in you will stay with you to complete the job by the day of Christ Jesus. Philippians 1:6 (CEB)

Confessions of the Pastor's Wife

Confessions of the Pastor's Wife

HEMMED IN

You hem me in behind and before, and you lay your hand upon me.

Psalm 139:5 (NIV)

I have always enjoyed bike riding. I love the sweet freedom that comes from hopping on a bike and cruising down the road. As a kid, the whole world suddenly opens up to you when you're on a bike. As an adult, I can now turn even a mundane trip to the grocery store into an aerobic workout!!

When my husband and I first started bike riding with our boys, there were some important rules we set down. First, no one gets onto a bike without a helmet. Second, no one crosses an intersection until they hear Mommy or Daddy yell, "Clear!" Generally, if the four of us are out together, one adult is in the lead and the other in the rear, hemming the boys in the middle.

The problem is, when I'm out riding alone with the boys, I cannot be both before and behind them. I have to pick one spot. If I ride before them, I can lead the way, call back when cars are approaching from the front, and get to busy intersections first. However, I can't see cars coming up from behind, I can't monitor where the boys are in the road, and the boys have a harder time hearing me call to them.

If I ride behind them, I can see and hear cars approaching both in front and behind, I can monitor their positions in the road,

Confessions of the Pastor's Wife

and my voice carries a bit farther. However, the boys have a tendency to zoom ahead and reach intersections before I do. And, if a car approaches too quickly from the front, I'm not there to immediately intercede, nor am I able to give directions to where we're going.

Ideally, I need to be in both places at once!!

This dilemma always reminds me of the fact that God is actually able to go both before us and behind us in our daily living, and I am so grateful for that! I rest assured knowing that if I am behind my boys, God is in front, and vice versa. Moreover, God is both leading us forward in our lives and watching our backs at the same time!

God goes before us—leading, directing, preparing the path, making sure the intersections are clear before we cross. And, God goes behind us—encouraging us onward, watching our progress, helping us out of scrapes along the way, not letting us fall behind, and standing between us and our past.

As if that's not incredible enough, God also walks right beside us every moment of every day. And sometimes, when we need it most, He has the ability to pick us up and carry us.

It's so comforting to know that God constantly surrounds us!

Dear God, thank you hemming me in. Help me to remember that no matter what my day brings, you go before, behind, and beside me all the way.

Scripture Bytes

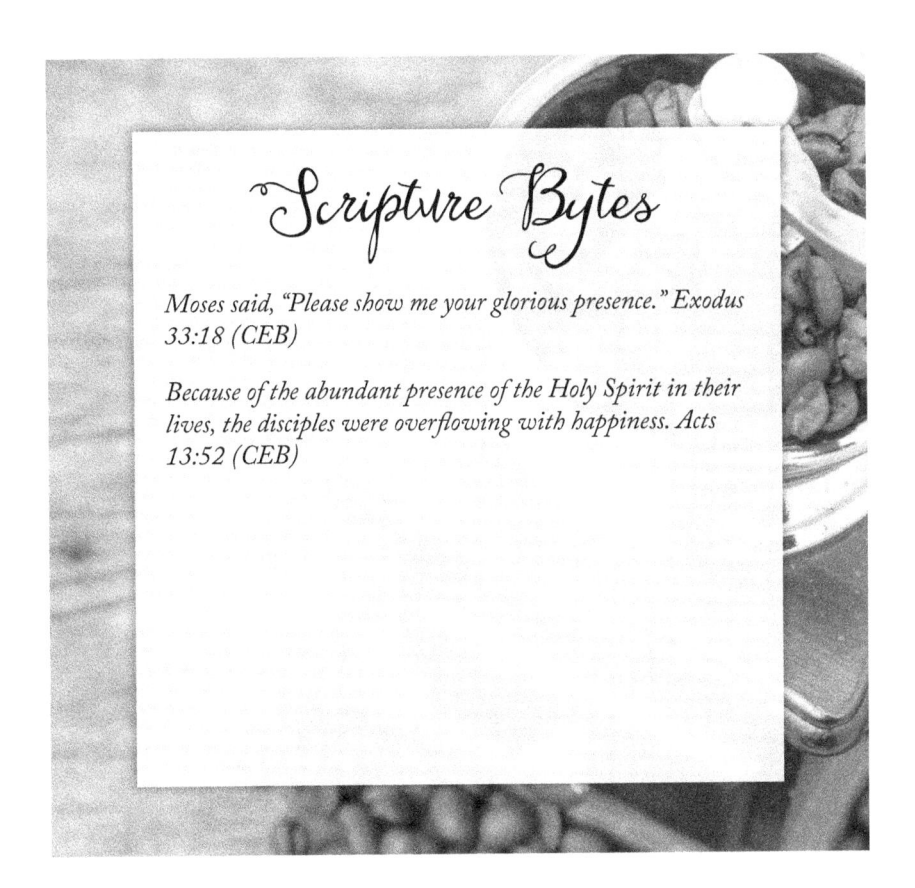

Moses said, "Please show me your glorious presence." Exodus 33:18 (CEB)

Because of the abundant presence of the Holy Spirit in their lives, the disciples were overflowing with happiness. Acts 13:52 (CEB)

Confessions of the Pastor's Wife

Confessions of the Pastor's Wife

SEEING GOD IN THE MIDST OF AN EPIC FAIL

Praise the Lord! He is good. God's love never fails. Praise the God of all gods. God's love never fails. Praise the Lord of lords. God's love never fails.

Psalm 136:1-3 (CEV)

For three years, I desperately tried to get a teaching position in my children's school district. We live in a small rural community and the school is two blocks from our house. I thought teaching there would be perfect. The boys and I would have the same schedule, we wouldn't need childcare, and I could be close by them every day.

When I secured my second job interview with the district, I thought, "This is it!" I prepared myself for the interview, going over questions and answers in my mind. I prayed continuously, asking God to make me appear favorable in the eyes of the hiring committee. I felt confident, allowing myself a vision of the future with me in that position. Everything I'd desired for the past three years would finally be coming to fruition! I couldn't wait to get started!

Confessions of the Pastor's Wife

Despite my preparedness, despite my prayers, I was less than my best throughout the interview. Ready answers weren't there. Important points failed to manifest themselves at the forefront of my mind. I remember at one point, about halfway through, actually thinking *Wow! I am totally bombing this!* as my mouth was responding to a question. I walked out of the interview room dazed and reeling. What had just happened? I found myself looking to the heavens, asking, "God, where were you?!" I had just had another "Epic Fail."

Walking home, I felt ashamed, wary of facing my family that eagerly awaited good news. I felt sad, depressed, and unworthy. I was angry. I had just finished reading a book about prayer in which I encountered story after story of God's amazing acts of power and might in the lives of the faithful who turned to him. Where was that power and might for me? Why wasn't God acting on *my* behalf? He knew how much this meant. He knew how much I wanted and longed for this. So why did he sit back and let me fail? How did this happen?

As I was praying that night, letting God have it, I felt the Spirit move in the quiet of my heart.

Lying in bed, surrounded by all of those awful feelings, I realized that the "Epic Fail" moments in life are the ones where we truly test and grow our trust in God. It's in our "Epic Fail" moments that we ask ourselves: *Does God really have a plan? Can God make something good out of this? Is God going to see me through this failure?* Answering those questions requires us to dig down deep into the very marrow of our spiritual bones. And if we can answer with even the feeblest "Yes," then it forces us to relinquish our feelings of bitterness, despair, injustice, and self-pity.

We can't hold on and wallow in negativity if we sense a bigger and better picture. If we answer "yes" to God and his sovereignty,

Confessions of the Pastor's Wife

then we have to trust, and trust can often feel like a free fall from 50,000 feet.

Over time, God has shown me that not getting that job was for my own benefit. He had a bigger plan. Although I don't always know where we're going on the grand map of life, I trust that God has the path laid out. I know that there will be other "Epic Fail" moments in my life. That's just part of living. But I also know this, regardless of what the future holds, God's love never fails.

Most loving and gracious God, thank you for walking down every path with me. Thank you for being there in my success and in my failure. Help me to trust in you. Take all of my Epic Failures and use them for your glory.

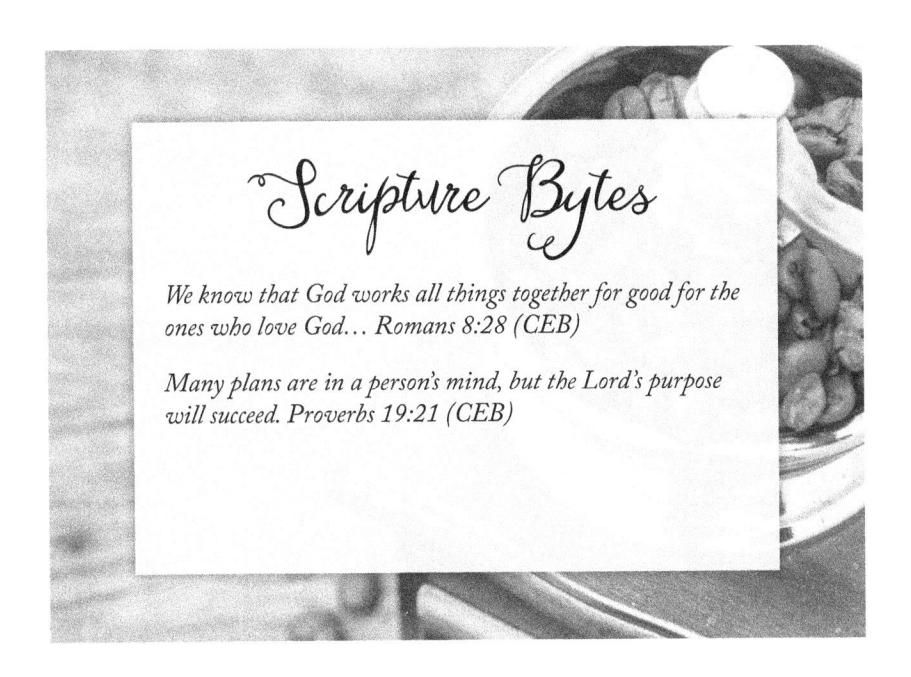

Scripture Bytes

We know that God works all things together for good for the ones who love God… Romans 8:28 (CEB)

Many plans are in a person's mind, but the Lord's purpose will succeed. Proverbs 19:21 (CEB)

Confessions of the Pastor's Wife

Confessions of the Pastor's Wife

BEING AN ACTIVE LISTENER

Obey God's message! Don't fool yourselves by just listening to it. If you hear the message and don't obey it, you are like people who stare at themselves in a mirror and forget what they look like as soon as they leave. But you must never stop looking at the perfect law that sets you free. God will bless you in everything you do, if you listen and obey, and don't just hear and forget.

James 1:22-25 (CEV)

Have you ever heard of the term *active listening*? I remember talking about this quite a bit in my undergrad Interpersonal Communications course. Active listening goes beyond simply hearing what someone has to say to being actively engaged with the speaker throughout the conversation. It's looking at someone while they're speaking, making eye contact, nodding your head, and giving verbal reinforcement and encouragement. Active listening tells the speaker:

- You are important to me
- I value your feelings and thoughts
- I respect you
- I understand you

Confessions of the Pastor's Wife

When we actively listen to someone, our actions demonstrate that we have received the message loud and clear. Our response to what the speaker has said shows that the speaker has been heard.

As the mother of two young boys, I truly appreciate the concept of active listening. I've found that my boys can hear quite a lot. For instance, they hear, "Go wash your hands and come to the table for dinner." But their continued playing or watching television five minutes after the fact tells me that they weren't really listening.

Similarly, we can hear God calling us to something, but our response to that call will prove whether or not we are actively listening.

Take this story of King Saul for example. In 1 Samuel 15, God sends Saul off on a conquering mission with specific instructions NOT to take any plunder from the attack. Saul hears the Lord's command, but does exactly the opposite. Saul takes the plunder from the attack in order to "make a generous sacrifice to the Lord," despite direct instruction that nothing should be saved. Samuel, God's prophet, comes to Saul and asks him, "Why didn't you listen to the Lord?"

Saul replies, "But, I did listen."

Samuel then points out the overwhelming evidence to the contrary. Saul tries to justify his actions, telling Samuel that the plunder was to be a thanksgiving offering to the Lord. Samuel's response:

> *"Tell me," Samuel said. "Does the Lord really want sacrifices and offerings? No! He doesn't want your sacrifices. He wants you to obey him."*
>
> *1 Samuel 15:22*

Confessions of the Pastor's Wife

When God calls us, He wants us to be active listeners. He wants to see that he is important to us, that he is valued and respected above all things, and—he wants to know by our obedient response that we understand him. If we are actively listening to God, then we are following his commands.

Here are a few steps to help you actively listen to God this week:

- **Set aside some time each day to focus your thoughts on God.** This can be during a commute, while walking or jogging, in the midst of your morning shower, or while sipping your first cup of coffee.

- **Ask God to speak to you about your day.** Perhaps you're in the middle of a situation that you're unsure how to handle. Maybe you're struggling with a decision, or trying to process something unexpected. Ask God for wisdom and understanding.

- **Act on what you hear.** Often, we know what God is asking us to do, we just don't always want to do it. This week, work on acting on what God is saying to you, regardless of how you feel about it.

- **Give God thanks and praise.** Thank God for what he has done and what he will do. Even if God's message doesn't seem clear to you, praise him for being there in the midst of your situation. Thank him for the clarity that will come in time.

Dear God, thank you for always being an active listener in my life. Help me this week to actively listen to you.

Scripture Bytes

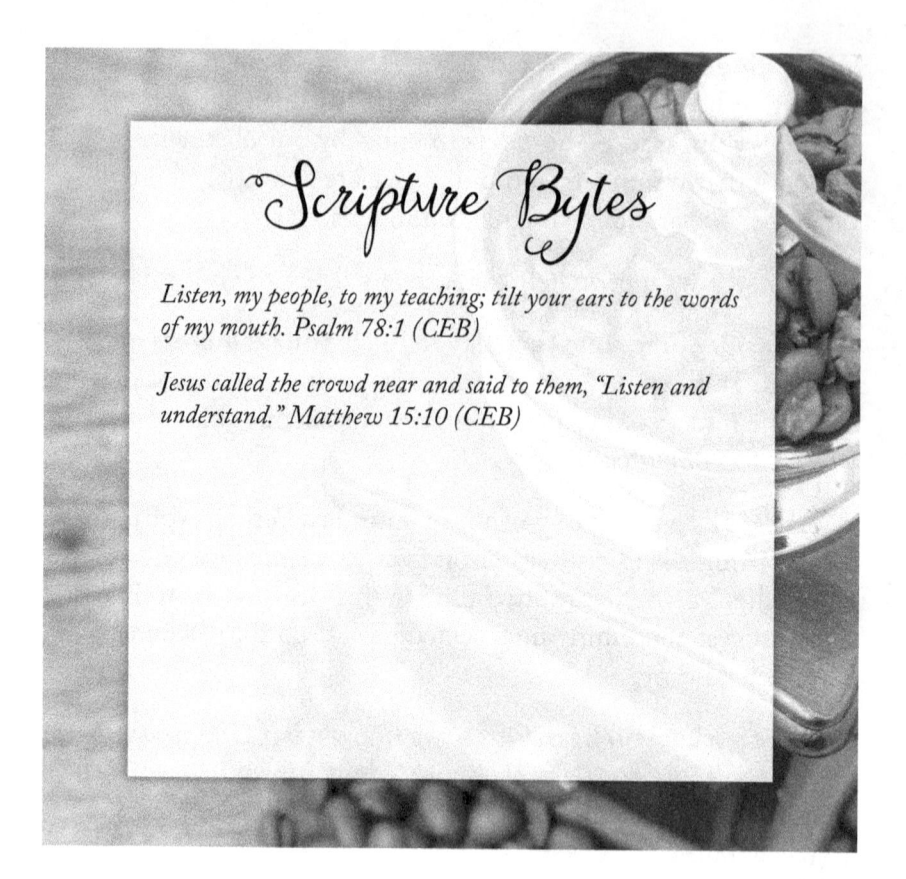

Listen, my people, to my teaching; tilt your ears to the words of my mouth. Psalm 78:1 (CEB)

Jesus called the crowd near and said to them, "Listen and understand." Matthew 15:10 (CEB)

Confessions of the Pastor's Wife

SEED-PLANTING DAYS

I know the plans I have for you, declares the Lord; they are plans for peace, not disaster, to give you a future filled with hope.

Jeremiah 29:11 (CEB)

I remember one morning a few years ago when I was dreading going to work. I felt like my time could be much better spent in the confines of my own home, cleaning, doing laundry, and reading my Bible. Grudgingly, I walked into the workroom to make some copies and noticed the look on the face of one of the teachers. Something told me to stop. She needed to talk and she needed some spiritual encouragement.

In that moment, I realized that God had placed me right there, right then, to fulfill a purpose. A few minutes earlier I had been asking myself, "Why, exactly, am I here today?" And in that hushed conversation, God showed me why, *exactly*, he had put me there.

When God calls us, there is something specific and meaningful he wants us to do. It might not seem very meaningful at the time, but some days are seed-planting days and some days are harvest days. Regardless of which day you're waking up to, I bet that God has something in mind for you to do.

Confessions of the Pastor's Wife

Moses was called to lead the Israelites out of Egypt—a harvest day if there ever was one! Jeremiah was called to speak the words God would place in his mouth—lots and lots of seed-planting days ahead. Esther was called to save her people—great big harvest! Ruth was called to love in faith—seed planting that established the line of David.

For me, most of my days seem to be of the seed-planting variety. I rarely see the "big picture" God has in mind. However, I firmly believe that God does indeed have a master plan. And in my prayer and Scripture time each morning, I ask God to place me smack in the middle of it.

Some days, my task is clear. I hear God calling me to write a note of encouragement, have a conversation with a friend or co-worker, offer a hug to a struggling student, write a blog post, sponsor a mission project...

Other days I don't hear anything, but I do not doubt that God is moving all the same. It's that *prevenient grace* of God moving through our lives, whether we are aware of it or not.

In our task-driven, goal-obsessed, results-oriented, data-driven culture, it's easy to forget that God has a multitude of tasks he will call us to throughout our lives. We focus on one big thing and strategically make a plan to achieve it. The reality is that life is much more fluid than that. We might begin our day with one agenda and find, upon awaking, that God has drawn out a completely different one.

And even if we are focused on that one giant task/dream/plan we feel God calling us to, God's probably not going to take us there in one straight shot. God called his people out of Egypt and into the Promised Land, but there were over forty years of smaller tasks to be completed before that harvest came to be. The people weren't ready for the big harvest yet. They needed to learn who God was. They needed to learn to trust in God, to honor him, to worship him, to LOVE him. They needed those forty-plus years to become *the people of God.*

In determining the big tasks God is calling us to do in our lives, we have to be open to the smaller tasks God calls us to each day. Jesus didn't tell Peter upon their first meeting, "You're going to lead my church in Jerusalem someday." Instead, he simply said, "Follow me. Put one foot in front of the other and walk along my path."

Jeremiah 29:11 is one of my favorite go-to verses. In this passage, the Lord assures the people of Israel that he has plans for them, and they're all good.

It's reassuring to me to know that God doesn't have just one plan for my life, he has PLANS! Moreover, those *plans* (note the plural) are good. They are infused with hope that springs from the great love of an eternal God. They are a promise carved into our souls of a prosperous future we cannot see. But God sees it. God knows it. God planned it. And God is building it.

So, what is God calling us to this day? To follow him. To trust him. To hope in him. To walk with him. You might not even see the seeds you're planting today. It doesn't matter. Trust that God has placed you exactly where he needs you to be.

Dear God, I know that you have plans for my life. Help me to listen to you, so that I may follow in your lead. Help me to delight in planting the seeds for your harvest, regardless of how small they may seem to me.

Scripture Bytes

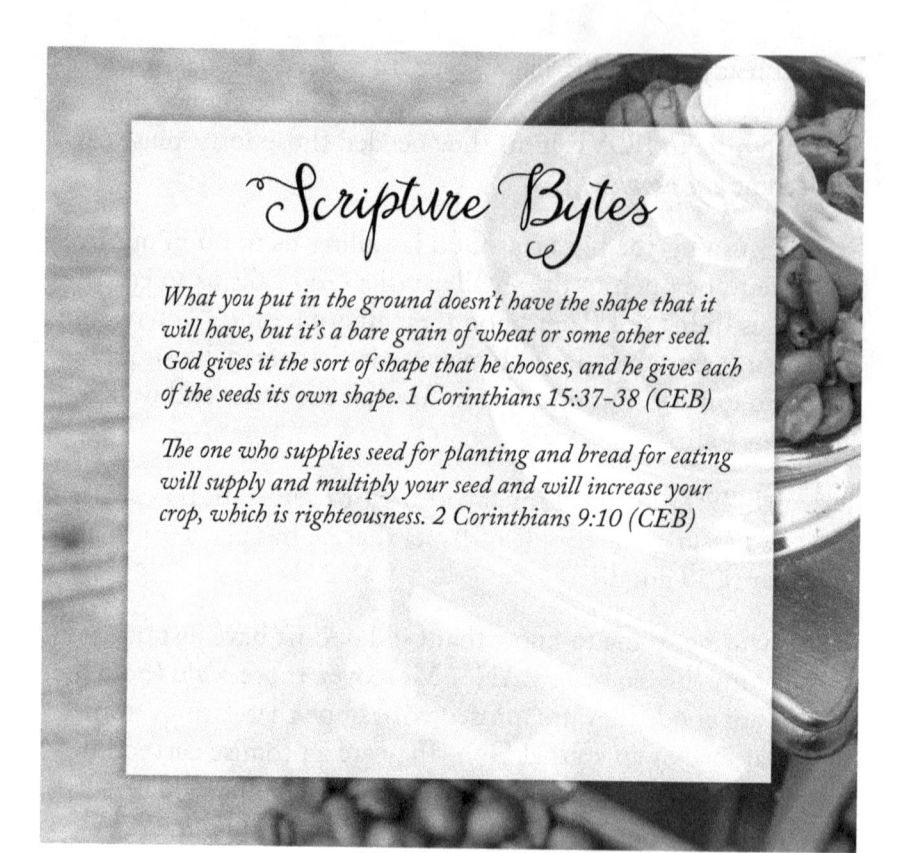

What you put in the ground doesn't have the shape that it will have, but it's a bare grain of wheat or some other seed. God gives it the sort of shape that he chooses, and he gives each of the seeds its own shape. 1 Corinthians 15:37-38 (CEB)

The one who supplies seed for planting and bread for eating will supply and multiply your seed and will increase your crop, which is righteousness. 2 Corinthians 9:10 (CEB)

Confessions of the Pastor's Wife

THE MIGHTY OAKS

They will be called mighty oaks, a planting of the Lord for the display of his splendor.

Isaiah 61:5 (NIV)

My husband enjoys woodworking. He has built a variety of things, from our dining room table to our dog house, and even a doll crib for our niece. His building projects always begin with a careful selection of wood. He spends hours (well, it seems like hours to me) studying the different types of wood available. Then, once he has selected the type of wood to use, he goes through the stack, piece by piece, looking for boards that are unblemished, even, and free of knots.

In general, my husband prefers working with oak. It is hard and strong with a great deal of natural beauty that needs little in the way of a cosmetic makeover. Although it's more expensive than other woods, its strength and beauty stand the test of time.

As children of God, we are made to be mighty oaks. Our Master Gardener infuses us with his strength and beauty. He prunes, weeds, and even sometimes transplants us so that we can withstand the test of time. When we keep our focus on God, we have the ability to withstand all that life throws at us.

Confessions of the Pastor's Wife

We can stand in the face of adversity because God gives us his unsurpassing strength.

As we walk in the Lord, as we grow deeper into him, he is able to keep us on an even keel. In God, we are steadfast. We don't have to spend our lives bouncing around from one thing to the next, searching for the next best thing. We have the best thing and God will lead us steadily onward.

Furthermore, in God, we have little need for a cosmetic makeover. Through Christ's sacrifice on the cross, we are able to come before the Lord without blemish, our sin washed clean in the blood of the Lamb.

As a mighty oak planted for the Lord, we reflect his splendor when we remain faithful to him, when we walk in his ways, when we obey his commands and when we show his love to others. We are Christ's keepsakes, spreading his love and teaching his commands, from generation to generation.

Gracious God, you have made me a mighty oak. Help me to reflect your splendor and majesty. Make me strong so that I may withstand all the storms of this life.

Confessions of the Pastor's Wife

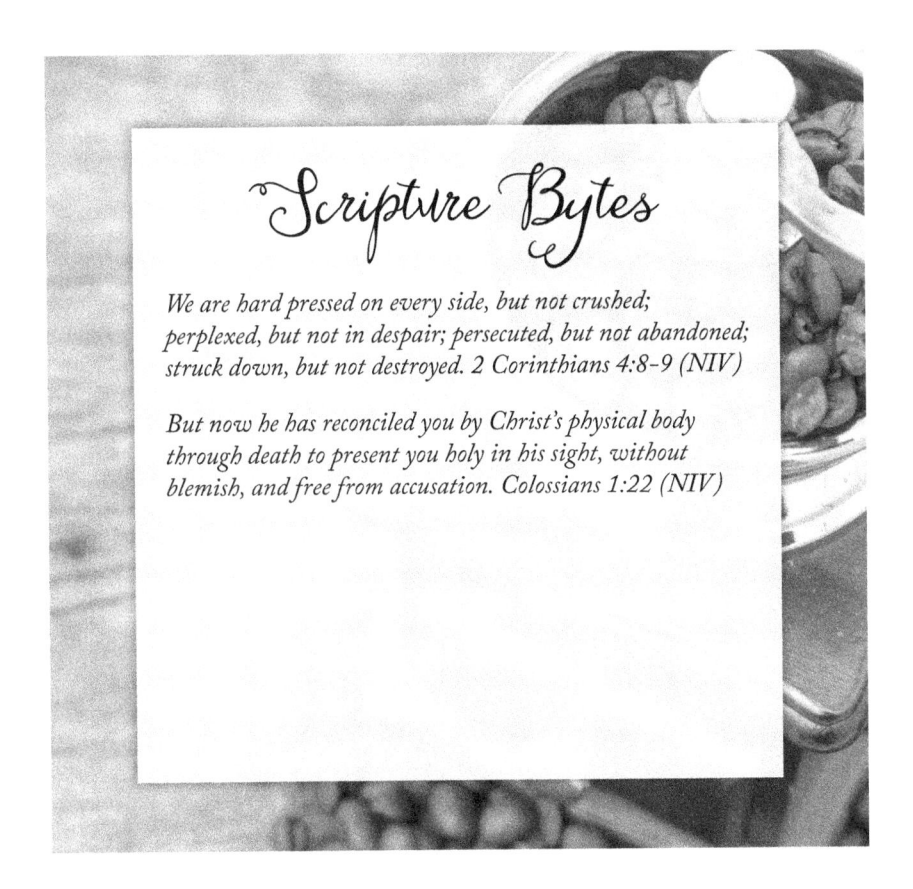

Scripture Bytes

We are hard pressed on every side, but not crushed; perplexed, but not in despair; persecuted, but not abandoned; struck down, but not destroyed. 2 Corinthians 4:8-9 (NIV)

But now he has reconciled you by Christ's physical body through death to present you holy in his sight, without blemish, and free from accusation. Colossians 1:22 (NIV)

Confessions of the Pastor's Wife

Confessions of the Pastor's Wife

BIRD FEEDER TRANSFORMATION

Do not conform to the pattern of this world, but be transformed by the renewing of your mind. Then you will be able to test and approve what God's will is—his good, pleasing, and perfect will.

Romans 12:2 (NIV)

This past winter, we got a bird feeder for Christmas. My husband planted the feeder right outside our front window so our boys could easily bird watch. Our youngest son ran to the closet and brought out a folding chair, setting it up in front of the window. He sat and watched the bird feeder with excited anticipation. Twenty minutes later, the anticipation wavered. No birds.

Days passed. No birds.

Weeks went by. No birds.

As winter blew on, we stopped anticipating bird watching. Ironically, there were hundreds of birds flying around the backyard, starlings and crows, but they never managed to make it around front where the food in our feeder sat cold and forgotten. *What's wrong with them?* I thought. *Don't they know there's food right here?*

Confessions of the Pastor's Wife

The cold winds of winter gave way to the warmth of spring. And suddenly, one evening, I saw it. A glorious red cardinal was eating from our bird feeder. Soon, he was joined by another cardinal, and the boys and I watched with bated breath, marveling at their red tails, pointy yellow beaks, and nimble claws.

The cardinals came back, day after day. Soon they were joined by red-headed finches and quail. Even some orange-breasted robins decided to get in on the act. We loved looking at the vibrant colors of these birds and listening to their different calls.

In retrospect, it would have made much more sense to plant our bird feeder in the back of the house where all of the starlings and crows congregated for the winter. But, had we done that, we would have missed the beauty of the cardinals, finches, robins, and quail. And their beauty reminds me of the glorious transformation that takes place within us when we come and receive the great love of God.

We are transformed. No longer do we run with the rest of the world, digging and pecking for wealth, acceptance, power, success, and approval. Rather, we are transformed into vibrant and beautiful servants of God. We are set apart, not for our own glory, but to glorify God.

However, in order to receive this transformation, we have to come to God. We have to seek him out. Like our bird feeder sitting silent through the winter, God is there. He is waiting to feed us with his love, his grace, his mercy, his forgiveness, his peace, and his understanding. But, we have to come.

This week, take some time to think about transformation. In what areas of your life are you conforming to the world? How can you live a life that more vibrantly points to the great love of God?

Confessions of the Pastor's Wife

Dear God, feeder of souls, help me to receive your love, your grace, your mercy, your peace, your forgiveness, and your understanding. Transform me from this world into a beautiful and vibrant daughter of the King. Let my life reflect your glory and point the way to you for others.

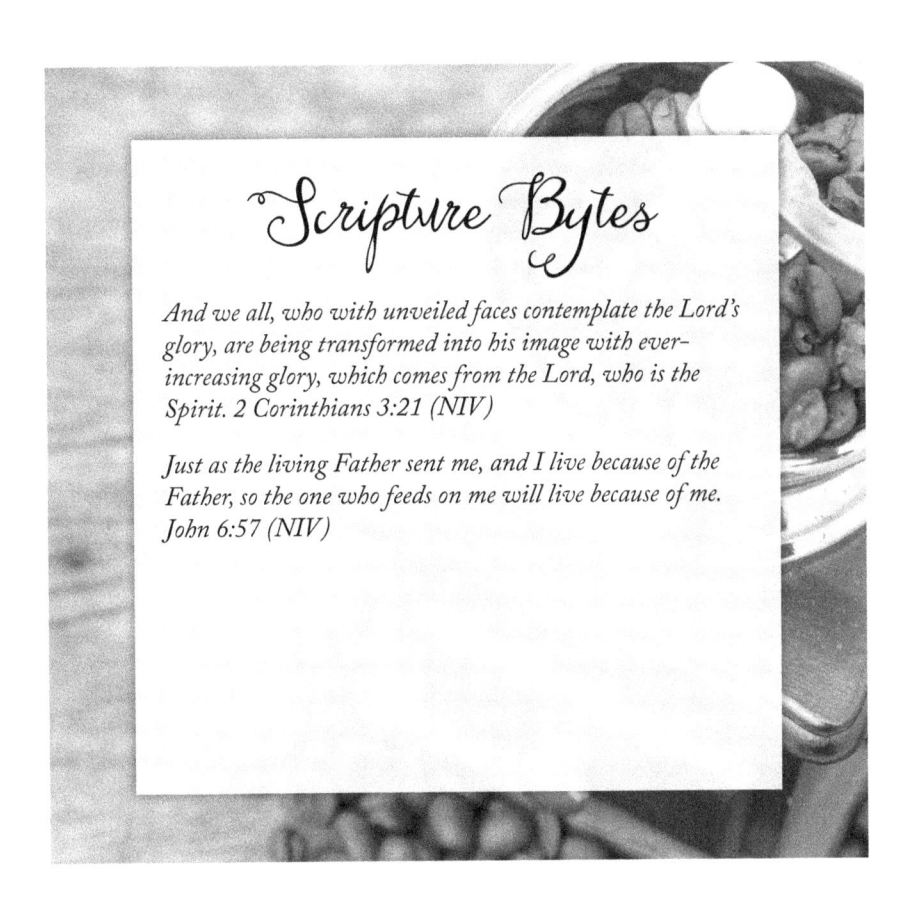

Scripture Bytes

And we all, who with unveiled faces contemplate the Lord's glory, are being transformed into his image with ever-increasing glory, which comes from the Lord, who is the Spirit. 2 Corinthians 3:21 (NIV)

Just as the living Father sent me, and I live because of the Father, so the one who feeds on me will live because of me. John 6:57 (NIV)

Confessions of the Pastor's Wife

Confessions of the Pastor's Wife

Kitchen Renovations

You were taught, with regard to your former way of life, to put off your old self, which is being corrupted by its deceitful desires; to be made new in the attitude of your minds; and to put on the new self, created to be like God in true righteousness and holiness.

Ephesians 4:22-24 (NIV)

Our parsonage kitchen is undergoing a renovation—the first one in over fifty years. While I am excited about the prospect of living in a house with a new kitchen (not very common for parsonage dwellers like us), I have to confess, I don't like change. I don't like digging around a plastic tub for my coffee sweetener. I don't like making sandwiches in the morning on the laundry room counter. I don't like the banging, and the crashing, and the never-ending dust that gets in my eyes and makes me sneeze.

Don't get me wrong. I'm not organized, and our house is always a mess. But, even in the mess, everything has its place. The books we're reading are always on the back of the "little" couch. The current mail is always on the far end of the kitchen peninsula. Coffee sweetener is never in a plastic tub full of herbs and spices.

I think if we're being honest, most of us don't like change. Our brains aren't wired for it. Our brains are designed to seek out patterns. It doesn't matter if the patterns are healthy or not, our brains thrive on routine. So when those routines are changed, we struggle. No wonder it's so hard to make the change to healthy eating!

However, change is an integral part of life. While our brains are seeking out a pattern for living, the current of life is constantly moving and shifting. Nothing stays the same. And really, that's a good thing. Think of your life as a giant heart monitor. If there's no change, there's no rhythm. And no rhythm equals a flat line—not so great for living.

In a sense, change is the pulse of life. It keeps us going. And while change can be difficult to accept, it provides us the opportunity to grow and evolve. Moreover, change allows God to work both in and through us to accomplish his purposes.

Understand that God does not always cause the changes in our lives. He can, when we ask him to intervene in situations. However, I believe it is dangerous to mistake God's sovereignty in this world with the defiance of human beings and the imperfections of the human body. I have seen too many mothers stand over the graves of their children to ever believe that God would purposefully bring about such a devastating loss.

Yet God is there, in the midst of even our most tragic changes, bringing comfort, peace, and strength when we feel we have none. Through the changes in our lives, God works within our souls to renew us, to strengthen us, and to bring us closer to him.

Changes can often lead to a renovation in our lives, if we are willing to let God work through them. Maybe a job loss leads to a new career opportunity you otherwise would never have pursued. Perhaps a scary health diagnosis prompts you to make positive changes in your lifestyle or pushes you to reconcile a

Confessions of the Pastor's Wife

fractured relationship. What if a move opens the door to new relationships and ministry opportunities?

Change happens, both planned and unplanned, positive and negative, well-received and fought against. Our lives are constantly under renovation. However, with God as our general contractor, we can make it through even the most unexpected changes.

This week, spend some time talking to God about the changes you are facing. Give God your fears about these changes. If you're angry, tell God. If you're hurting, tell God. Ask God for his peace to be with you. Trust that, whatever it is, God will see you through.

Dear God, change is hard. Often, I don't understand it. Help me to feel your presence as I walk down the path of change. Give me your strength and your peace as I move through the renovations of life.

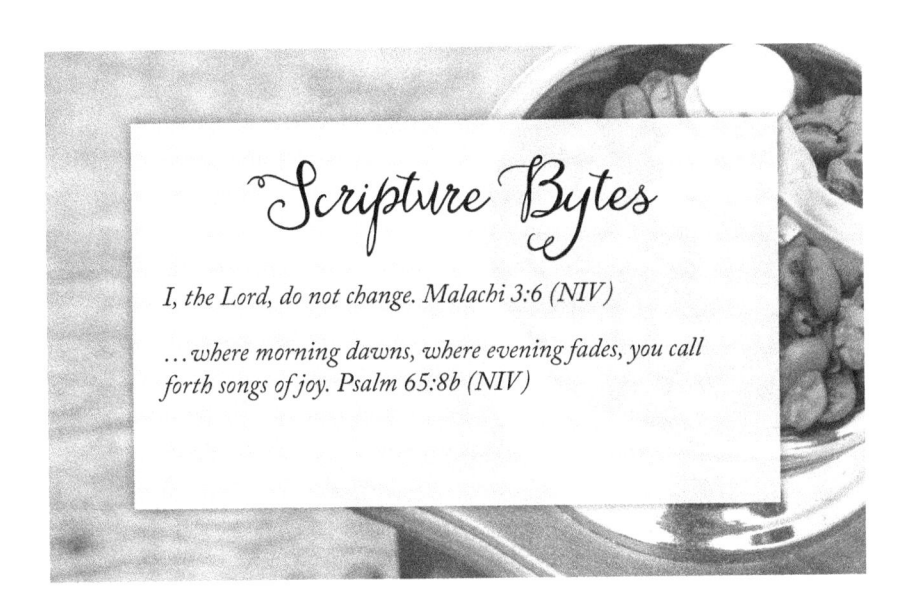

Scripture Bytes

I, the Lord, do not change. Malachi 3:6 (NIV)

…where morning dawns, where evening fades, you call forth songs of joy. Psalm 65:8b (NIV)

Confessions of the Pastor's Wife

Confessions of the Pastor's Wife

PRESSING ON

But one thing I do: forgetting what is behind and straining toward what is ahead, I press on toward the goal to win the prize for which God has called me heavenward in Christ Jesus.

Philippians 3:13-14 (NIV)

A few years ago, my boys came down with the stomach flu while we were visiting my parents. As it was impossible to drive the thirty-five miles back to our house, we hunkered down at Mom and Dad's—four pairs of hands for two grossly explosive kids. Around one o'clock in the morning, as my mom and I were on our hands and knees using flashlights to spot clean the carpets, the thought entered my mind that life is really just about endurance. You just endure one thing after another until you die and then go sit on a cloud in some ephemeral place to play a harp for eternity.

It was in that moment that God burst into my middle-of-the-night pity party and said, *Really? This is what you really believe?*

The truth is, life is about endurance, but not in that whiny self-pitying way we often make it out to be. Rather, as Paul writes, we endure life the way a marathon runner endures the rigors of a race. We "press on" toward our goal, whatever challenges life may throw our way. And we experience triumphant joy when we finally cross that finish line that marks the end of our race.

Confessions of the Pastor's Wife

At this point, you may be wondering what the goal of the race is. Simply put, our goal in life is to prepare the way for the Lord. God called us, his people, to go forth and show his love to the world. We are called to spread the good news that God loves us, that he has saved us, that he offers all humanity his mercy, and hope, and grace.

Pressing on means that we look beyond ourselves, our problems, our fears, our limitations, and our struggles in order to be the hands and feet of Christ to someone else. Pressing on means facing life's challenges without complaining or moping or throwing pity parties. In fact, when we press on toward the goal, we don't have time to mope and feel sorry for ourselves because we're so busy running the race God has placed before us.

People who truly grasp the concept of pressing on toward the goal are those who are actively engaged in spreading love. They are those who adopt families for Christmas, provide meals for those who are hungry, travel around the world to build wells, churches, and schools, and visit the sick and imprisoned. Those who truly grasp the concept of pressing on toward the goal are those people who are training for marathons in remembrance of loved ones and in the hope that their efforts will mean no other family has to fear when the doctor says the biopsy does not look good. They are the people who make time to listen to a friend in need, who find ways to bring cheer to those who are lonely or alone, or those who campaign for laws that will positively benefit children and the poor of our nation.

People who truly grasp the concept of pressing on toward the goal do so without regard for what other people might think, or the challenges and stumbling blocks placed along the path. Their eyes are focused ahead, laser-locked on the One who is cheering them onward.

Confessions of the Pastor's Wife

This week, take some time to consider those situations in your life where you feel like you simply "endure." How might you press on through those situations to show the love of God to others?

Dear God, help me to move from a spirit of endurance to one of hope and motivation. Help me to fix my eyes on you and press on toward the goal for which you have called me heavenward in Christ Jesus.

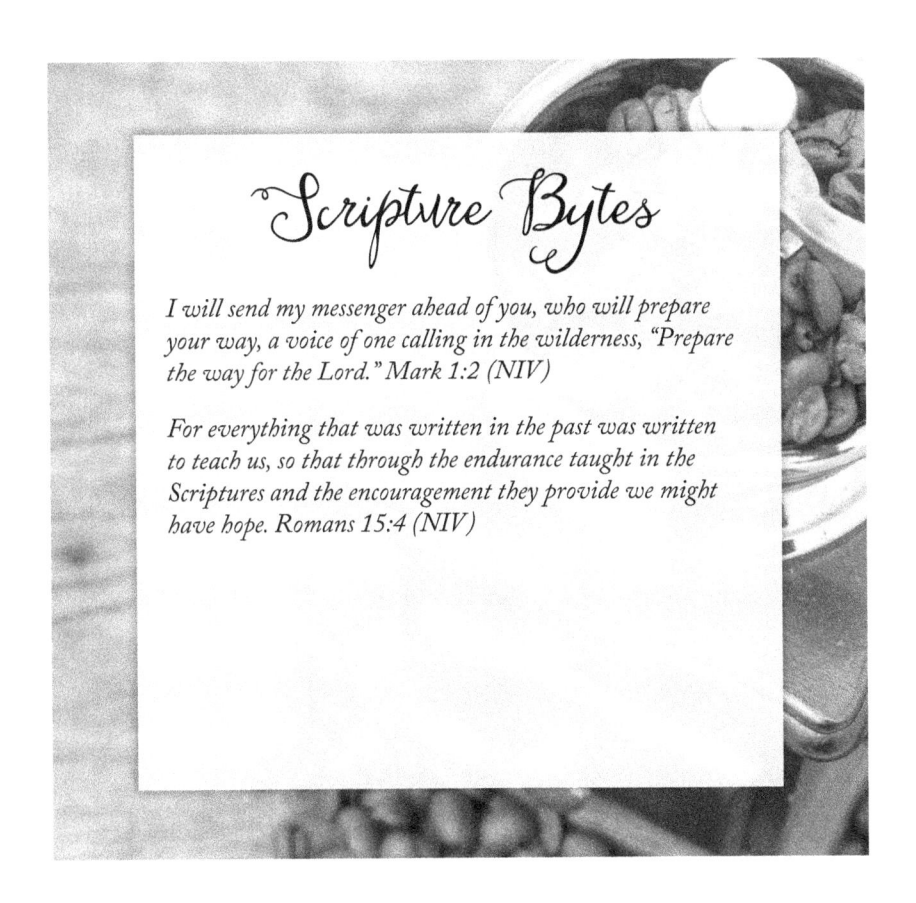

Scripture Bytes

I will send my messenger ahead of you, who will prepare your way, a voice of one calling in the wilderness, "Prepare the way for the Lord." Mark 1:2 (NIV)

For everything that was written in the past was written to teach us, so that through the endurance taught in the Scriptures and the encouragement they provide we might have hope. Romans 15:4 (NIV)

Confessions of the Pastor's Wife

Confessions of the Pastor's Wife

DON'T TRY SO HARD

See what kind of love the Father has given to us in that we should be called God's children, and that is what we are!

1 John 3:1 (CEB)

I am a people pleaser. I thrive on positive affirmation. If someone tells me I'm doing a job well, I will strive all the more to continue to earn that respect and "please" whoever is praising me. If someone is displeased with a job I am doing, I go out of my way to "prove" my worth.

I remember sitting in one of my first graduate school classes, listening to the professor talk about the high expectations the seminary had for student achievement. He told us not to expect to get As, that they were very hard to come by, and that a B in seminary was an indication of high quality work. I looked over at the woman sitting next to me and said, "I'm getting an A in this class."

As a former teacher, I always told my students that the grades themselves weren't important, it was what they learned that counted the most. However, as a pleaser, those grades were important to me. I equated earning an A with being successful.

Confessions of the Pastor's Wife

If I earned an A, then I had pleased the professor and was a "good student."

Unfortunately, I tend to carry this need to please into my relationship with God. I get caught up in the idea that I can earn God's approval and acceptance if I tithe, or teach Sunday school, or do service projects. The problem is, nothing I do ever seems to be good enough. When it comes to earning God's love, there's never an end to the endeavor. This is because God's love, God's pleasure, is not something that can ever be earned. There is nothing I can do to please God, because God is already pleased by me.

The truth is, God already loves me. He already loves you. God created us. He formed us in the womb. He loved us before we took our first breath. We are God's children, the work of his hands, created in his image to do the work he has set out for us. The work that we do isn't about earning God's love; rather, it's about showing God's love to others. Our giving, serving, and worshipping should be a direct response to God's love, not a precursor to it.

Time and again in Scripture God tells his people, "I don't want your sacrifices. I just want you, my children, to come to me!" The truth is, God has already done all of the work for us. God sent Christ, his Son, to wipe away every barrier that stood between us and him. God loved us so much that *he* saved us. God sacrificed a part of himself for us because we are his beloved creation. There is nothing we can do to earn his pleasure or his love. It's already there. We just have to accept it.

This week, spend some time reflecting on God's love for you.

- Do you believe that God loves you just as you are?

Confessions of the Pastor's Wife

- Can you accept that God loves you right now, regardless of how much you weigh, what job you have, how much money you give to the church, how many broken relationships you've had, or how often you go to church?

- Are you trying to earn God's love? If so, in what ways?

- How would your life look if you stopped trying to earn God's love? What would you do differently?

- Take a moment to still yourself before God. Listen for his gentle whisper. Hear him as he says, "I love you. I am pleased with you. Don't try so hard."

Dear God, thank you for your great love. Help me to see myself as a beloved daughter of the King. Help me to stop trying to earn your love, but instead, to show the great love you have for me to others.

Scripture Bytes

God so loved the world that he gave his only Son, so that everyone who believes in him won't perish, but will have eternal life. God didn't send his Son into the world to judge the world, but that the world might be saved through him. John 3:16-17 (CEB)

With what should I approach the Lord and bow down before God on high? Should I come before him with entirely burned offerings, with year-old calves? Will the Lord be pleased with thousands of rams, with many torrents of oil? Should I give my oldest child for my crime; the fruit of my body for the sin of my spirit? He has told you, human one, what is good and what the Lord requires from you: to do justice, embrace faithful love, and walk humbly with your God. Micah 6:6-8 (CEB)

Confessions of the Pastor's Wife

FREE FALLING WITH GOD

While Jesus was still speaking, some people came from the house of Jairus, the synagogue leader. "Your daughter is dead," they said. "Why bother the teacher anymore?" Overhearing what they said, Jesus told him, "Don't be afraid; just believe."

Mark 5:35-36 (NIV)

A few years ago, our family was planning an extensive vacation. We started planning it over a year in advance. We booked rooms, flights, tickets, and dining reservations. We read and discussed information from books, blogs, articles, and social media about our destination. We made lists of rides we wanted to ride, shows we wanted to see, and experiences we wanted to have. For a fun family vacation, this was turning into a lot of hard work. It dawned on me that if we spent any more time planning and preparing for this trip, we were going to ruin the entire experience. Our meticulous planning was taking away from the excitement, adventure, and enjoyment this trip was supposed to bring.

In our culture, we like plans. There are step-by-step planning guides for any endeavor you wish to undertake, whether it be planning a vacation, planning for college, planning for retirement, planning for marriage, or planning for a big family dinner. We thrive on plans.

Confessions of the Pastor's Wife

It's easy to get caught up in planning out our lives. We spend hours, days, sometimes even years, designing and cultivating our life plans. We like the plan. It's familiar. It's measurable. It's attainable. Yet one of the problems in planning out every moment of our lives is that we inadvertently shut God out. We rely on our plans like we would a safety harness, forgetting that God can do immeasurably more than we could ask or imagine or *plan*.

Sometimes, God wants us to let go of that safety harness and free fall into him. Free falling into God means putting all of our faith and trust in him, regardless of what the plan we've created says to do. God has a direction and purpose for each of us. Sometimes, that direction and purpose is contrary to the one we've established for ourselves.

When I was twenty, I had a plan. It was mapped out in a straight line, from my first teaching position to retirement at age sixty. A few years into that plan, God intervened. I took a drastic leap of faith and my plan was completely altered. I was free falling, and it terrified me. However, in the midst of the free fall, God provided for me in ways I never imagined. Not only was God's plan better than mine, in following God's plan, my faith grew and matured. By taking off the safety harness of my plan to free fall into God, I learned to trust him.

Plans are an important part of being successful. We need to set measurable and attainable goals for ourselves and our families. However, we also need to be willing to unhook our safety harness when God asks us to do something new. This week, think about an area of your life plan where God wants to make some changes. Perhaps God is asking you to give up a social group for a Bible study. Maybe God's calling you to give up a profitable career to work in the ministry. Could God be asking you to mend a fractured relationship, or give up something you've been saving for in order to send a needy child to school? Whatever it is, think about what it would take to free fall into God. And know this, once you unhook that safety harness, God is waiting to catch you.

Most loving and gracious God, I have many plans for my life. Help me this week to fully and completely yield those plans to you. Help me to unhook that safety harness so that I may fall into your strong and perfect arms.

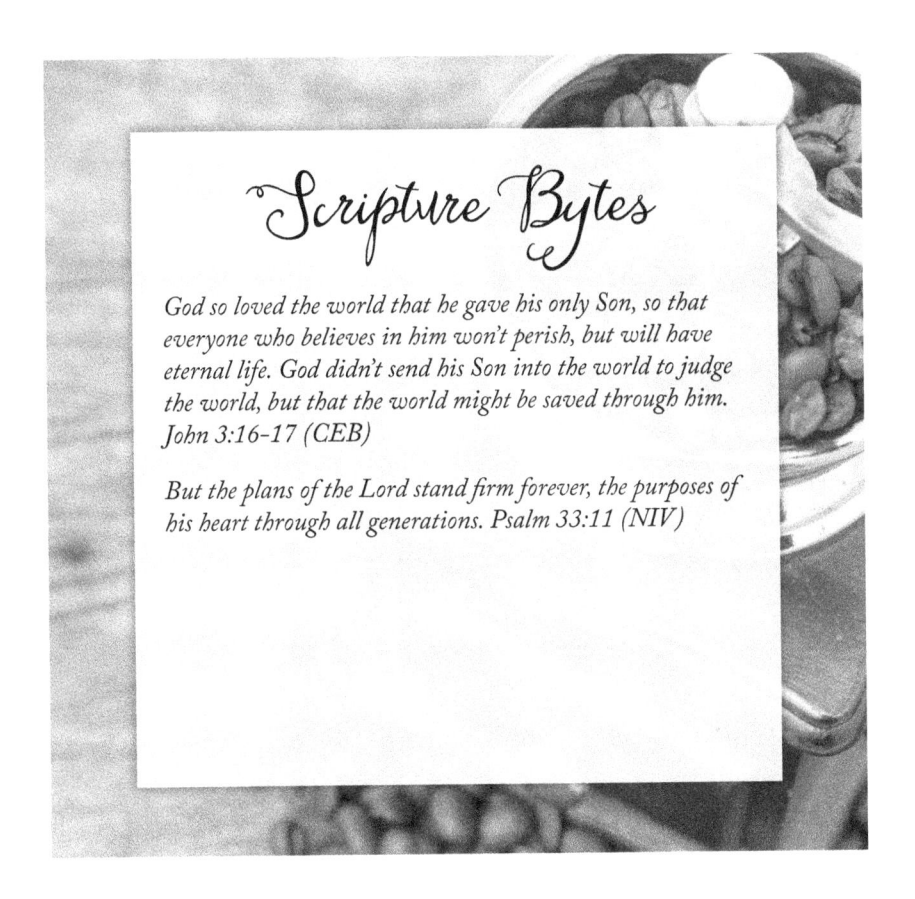

Scripture Bytes

God so loved the world that he gave his only Son, so that everyone who believes in him won't perish, but will have eternal life. God didn't send his Son into the world to judge the world, but that the world might be saved through him. John 3:16-17 (CEB)

But the plans of the Lord stand firm forever, the purposes of his heart through all generations. Psalm 33:11 (NIV)

Confessions of the Pastor's Wife

Confessions of the Pastor's Wife

DO WHAT YOU'RE SUPPOSED TO DO

Therefore, my loved ones, just as you always obey me, not just when I am present but now even more while I am away, carry out your own salvation with fear and trembling. God is the one who enables you both to want and to actually live out his good purposes.

Philippians 2:12-13 (CEB)

When I quit my full-time teaching job to focus on writing, it was with the intent of opening up more space in my life to do those things God had placed on my heart to do. I wanted to engage in more ministry and service-related activities. Do you know how many more ministry and service-related activities I engaged in? Nada. None. Zilch. Instead of focusing my time and resources on God's work, I found myself focusing on what everyone else should be doing, from politicians to my child's teachers. In my times of meditation and prayer during this period, I heard God saying to me: "Focus only on the work I have placed in front of you. Do what you're supposed to do."

The trouble was, I wanted to do everyone else's stuff, too. Let me explain...

Confessions of the Pastor's Wife

One weekend, my four-year-old niece was playing soccer. Well, she was *supposed* to be playing soccer. What she actually did was spend most of the game following her coach up and down the field, commenting on what everyone else was doing wrong. At one point, as a girl from the other team ran the ball toward a goal, I heard my niece's little voice say, "She's not supposed to do that! She's supposed to share!" And while that might have been true, it was not my niece's job to tell her that. At the end of the game, my niece came over to us, her face downcast. "I only scored three goals," she said. In focusing on what everyone else was or wasn't doing, my niece didn't play to her full potential.

The truth is, we adults rarely play to our full potential either. We're so focused on what everyone else is doing, or not doing, that we completely ignore the work God has put in front of us to do. We get so caught up in neighborhood gossip, workplace drama, and Facebook posts that we sometimes miss out on living our own lives. Moreover, we miss out on the opportunities God is giving us to do his work, which is the entire purpose of our being.

In the book of Philippians, Paul encouraged the Philippian church to continue in their work. "Press on," Paul told them. "Run the race God has set out for you." In order to run that race, we need to focus our eyes, our energy, our resources, and our time on those things God has asked us to do. If you're unsure as to what those things are, then ask God to remind you.

On the soccer field, as my niece struggled to stay focused on what she was supposed to do, our family called out words of encouragement from the sidelines. "Follow the ball! Get in there! You've got this! Keep going!" This week, know that God is telling you the same thing.

Confessions of the Pastor's Wife

God, I confess that I have not engaged in the work you have set out for me to do. I have been distracted, unfocused, and unengaged. Help me to set my eyes on you so that I may finish the race you have set before me.

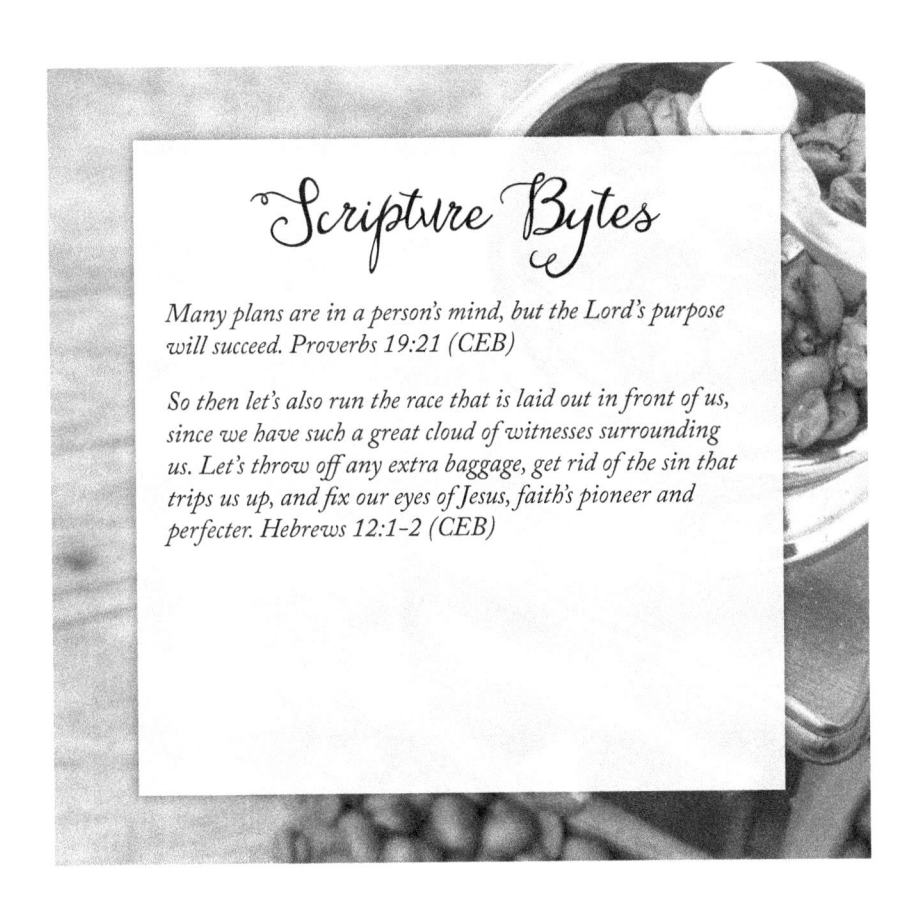

Scripture Bytes

Many plans are in a person's mind, but the Lord's purpose will succeed. Proverbs 19:21 (CEB)

So then let's also run the race that is laid out in front of us, since we have such a great cloud of witnesses surrounding us. Let's throw off any extra baggage, get rid of the sin that trips us up, and fix our eyes of Jesus, faith's pioneer and perfecter. Hebrews 12:1-2 (CEB)

Confessions of the Pastor's Wife

Confessions of the Pastor's Wife

LITTLE SIGNS

God is our refuge and strength, a help always near in times of great trouble. That's why we won't be afraid when the world falls apart, when the mountains crumble into the center of the sea.

Psalm 46:1-2a (CEB)

I must confess, sometimes I feel as if my most ardent prayers fall on deaf ears. It's so hard, in the midst of a crisis or storm, to see God anywhere in the situation. Our anger, anxieties, fears, and sorrows can swell around us, creating a tidal wave of emotion that threatens to engulf us completely.

I remember a sleepless night when my oldest was still a baby. He was a terrible sleeper. It was 4:15 a.m. I was exhausted. My alarm was set for 6 a.m. I hated being a parent. I fervently prayed for patience and peace, for the strength to endure and not plop my infant son onto the floor and leave him alone in the dark. Instead of finding the calm within the storm, I found tears—lots of them. But later that day, I also found good friends who shared in my struggles with being a mom. They reassured me and encouraged me. They told me it was okay.

There have been other moments in my life when I have desperately prayed for a sign of God's presence. I want a bold fork of lighting to come crashing down from the sky, reminding me that God is there, that he hears, that he cares. Often, I get little signs in unexpected places that tell me God is near.

Confessions of the Pastor's Wife

Not too long ago, I was facing a crisis. I was pounding my anger out on the pavement of a street, wondering where God was in the midst of this latest calamity. All of a sudden, I heard little paw steps behind me. *Go away,* I thought, as a little dog trotted up next to me. He didn't leave. Instead, this strange dog stayed with me over the course of the next few blocks, a little companion to my anger and fear. Sometimes he walked in front of me on the road, leading the way to a destination I couldn't see. Other times, he fell behind and frolicked in green grasses. When we passed his house, he veered off the path and to his front porch, welcomed home by his owner who was waiting by the door.

I couldn't help but think of the Israelites wandering through the desert so many years ago. God, in flame and smoke, went both before and behind them as they journeyed down an unknown path. They were confused, lost, sad, and terrified. And yet, God was with them the whole way. My unexpected furry companion that dark morning was a little sign of God's presence in my life. While I still didn't know where the road would ultimately lead, I knew God was there. And sometimes, that's just enough to keep our heads above water.

The truth is, our lives are never going to be easy. We will struggle, we will stumble, and we will even fall. We will experience grief, heartbreak, betrayal, fear, humiliation, pain, and injustice. Yet God has promised us this—he will never abandon or forsake his children. God gives us little signs of his presence. We just have to move out of our darkness in order to see them.

This week, take a look around your life. Where is God showing you his presence? Is it in the friend bringing a dinner by because she knows you're experiencing sickness or loss? Is it in the faithful four-legged companion who is always right by your side? Is it in the laughter of your children as they play? Is it in the warm embrace of someone you love? Give thanks to God for these signs of his presence.

Moreover, find a way to show someone else God's love and faithfulness this week. Send a note of encouragement to a friend who is struggling. Offer to babysit one day for a single mom. Send some flowers to someone who could use an unexpected gift. Pay for the drink of the person behind you in the coffee shop line.

Whatever you're facing right now, know that God has not abandoned you. Know, too, that sometimes God asks us to be his hands and feet.

Dear God, thank you for your promise to never abandon or forsake me. Please show me your presence in a real and tangible way. Help me to reach beyond myself in order to show others your presence, as well.

Scripture Bytes

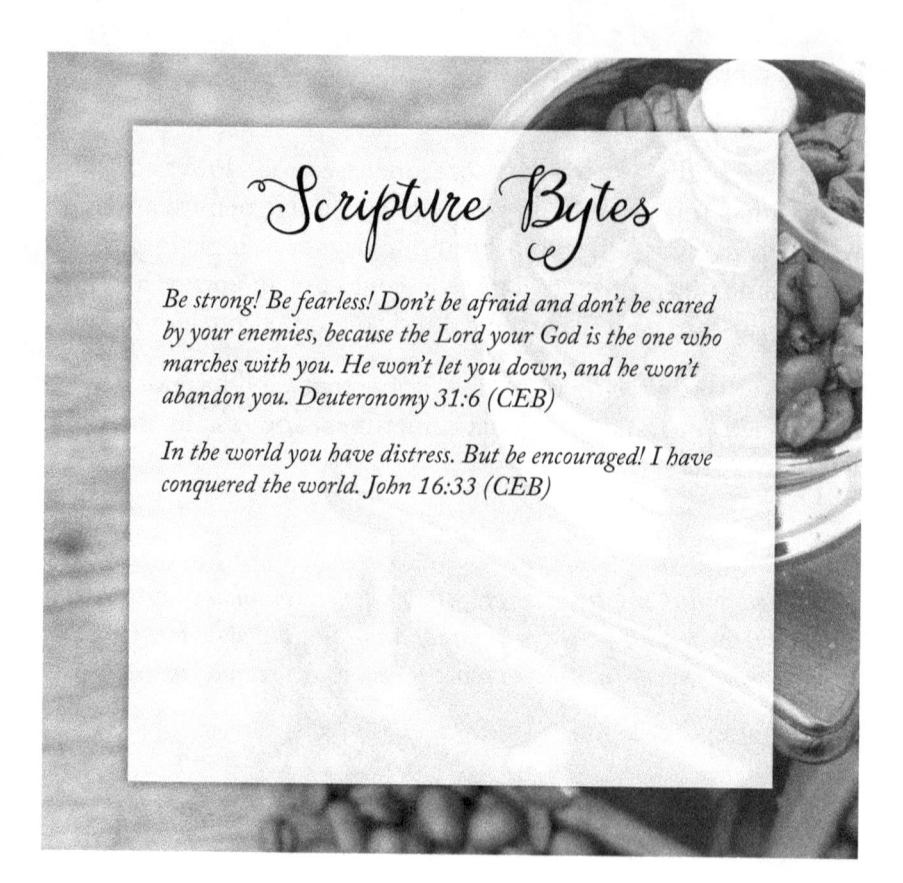

Be strong! Be fearless! Don't be afraid and don't be scared by your enemies, because the Lord your God is the one who marches with you. He won't let you down, and he won't abandon you. Deuteronomy 31:6 (CEB)

In the world you have distress. But be encouraged! I have conquered the world. John 16:33 (CEB)

Confessions of the Pastor's Wife

FAITH AND TRUST

> *...faith is dead when it doesn't result in faithful activity. Someone might claim, "You have faith and I have action." Instead, I'll show you my faith by putting it into practice in faithful action.*
>
> James 2:17-18 (CEB)

When my oldest son was an infant, he developed a respiratory infection. One night he had a coughing fit and, at one point, gave a great gasp. My husband, who had been sleeping, sat bolt upright. I held my son until the coughing subsided and I laid him back down to sleep, but I couldn't let him go. I lay down at the foot of our bed, my ear pressed close to our son's playpen, listening to him breathe. After about ten minutes of this, I felt God gently pulling me away.

Before I laid my son to sleep, I had prayed that God would watch over him through the night. In that moment of fear and anxiety, God brought the words of that prayer back to my mind. In the darkness, it dawned on me that in order for God to watch over him through the night, I had to let him go. I realized that in order to have faith in God, I first had to trust God.

There is a distinct connection between faith and trust. The apostle James makes this connection when he talks about the importance of faith in action. It is only when we trust in God that we can act on our faith. Scripture abounds with stories of people actively trusting in their faith. Abraham and Sarah trust in God's promises and faithfully pack up and move to another land. Noah trusts in God's message and builds an ark on dry ground. Samuel trusts in God's wisdom and anoints a shepherd boy as king. Mary trusts in God's revelation and has a child before she is married. When we trust God, we live by faith.

Often, we let our anxieties and fears overpower our trust in God. We are faithless because we are afraid. In the Gospels, Peter asks Jesus if he can walk on the water with him. At one point, Peter wavers in his trust and begins to sink. He cries out to Jesus for help and Jesus asks him, "Where is your faith?" Peter's faith waned as his fears overpowered his trust.

It is easy to lose faith in this world. We see and experience so much hurt, violence, oppression, and injustice that we begin to wonder if God is there at all. Fear breeds doubt and mistrust. It is one of the enemy's greatest tools. If we lose our trust, then we will most likely lose our faith. The good news for us is that God is there. He is standing right next to us in the midst of the sea of our fears. He is asking us the same question Jesus asked Peter so long ago. "Where is your faith?"

In order to fully trust in God, to live out a life of active faith, we must release our fears to the only One big enough to conquer them. We have to trust God enough to let him have all of those things that keep us from trusting in him. And when we let those fears and anxieties go, we see that God's goodness is all around. It's in the healing that comes to friends who have been ill. It's in the warmth of time spent with family and friends. It's in the beauty of a sunrise or sunset. It's in the joy of seeing a hungry child fed. It's in placing the final brick for a new school in an impoverished land.

Confessions of the Pastor's Wife

When we trust in God, we are able to go out into a world that is desperately crying for help, and we are able to bring God's light and love to those in need. When we trust in God, we live by faith, and the life we live is active and purposeful. This week, spend some time laying your fears and anxieties before God. Work to let go of those things that are keeping you from trusting him. Work on developing an active faith.

Faithful God, I confess that I do not trust you with my whole heart. I am afraid. I am anxious. Please help me to surrender my fears and anxieties to you. Help me to feel your loving embrace and to confidently go forth in faith.

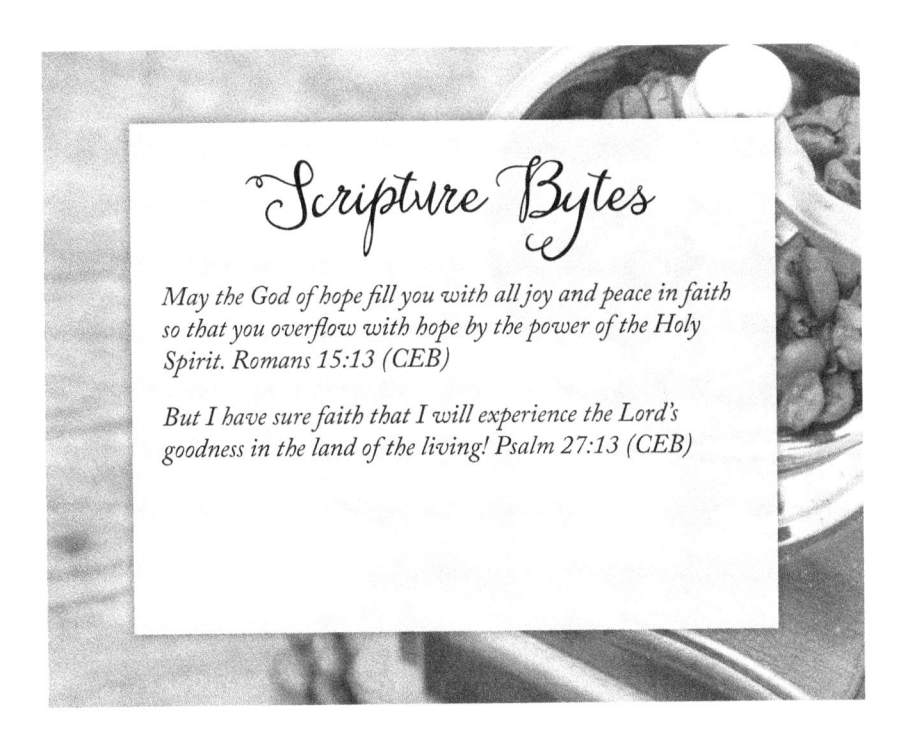

Scripture Bytes

May the God of hope fill you with all joy and peace in faith so that you overflow with hope by the power of the Holy Spirit. Romans 15:13 (CEB)

But I have sure faith that I will experience the Lord's goodness in the land of the living! Psalm 27:13 (CEB)

Confessions of the Pastor's Wife

Confessions of the Pastor's Wife

LEGACIES

I'm grateful to God whom I serve as my ancestors did. I constantly remember you in my prayers day and night...I'm reminded of your authentic faith, which first lived in your grandmother Lois and your mother Eunice. I'm sure that this faith is also inside you.

2 Timothy 1: 3, 5 (CEB)

Saturday mornings are pretty laid back in our house. We rarely rush around, but rather, spend time lazily pursuing our own activities. On one recent Saturday, I was watching my boys. My oldest was curled up on the floor with his nose firmly planted in a book, while my youngest was actively constructing a fort out of the sofa cushions. As I looked at them, I saw my husband and I—my husband in my youngest son's industrious pursuit and myself in my oldest son's love of reading. I started thinking about how much we pass on to the next generation, sometimes without even knowing it.

We are all a product of the generations that have gone before us. We all have a legacy that we carry. For some, it is a legacy of hurt, of anger, of mistrust, of abuse, or maybe even of addiction. Even though we may carry these negative legacies within us, we are not obligated to pass them on.

The thing about legacies is that we can choose, here and now, what we leave behind for the next generation. Are we going to

Confessions of the Pastor's Wife

burden our children with our emotional baggage? Are we going to saddle them with our fears and insecurities? Or are we going to give them something they can value?

When I was a girl, Sunday afternoons were spent around the dining room table eating pot roast and discussing faith. My parents actively sought to engage my sister and me in conversations about Scripture we had studied in Sunday school or the message the pastor had delivered. I learned a lot around that table. Most importantly, I learned how to have an active faith.

My dad's active involvement in faith was passed down to him from his parents. My grandfather carefully read and studied Scripture each morning. When I stayed with my grandparents during the summer, my grandfather included me in that Bible study. From generation to generation, the message was clear: faith is a central component of life.

One of the most important things I can pass onto my children is legacy of faith in Jesus Christ. I want my boys to know Christ, to follow him, to live lives in service to him. For me, that's the legacy that matters most.

In 2 Timothy, Paul writes to Timothy to remind him of the faith he has that has been passed down to him from his grandmother and mother. *You come from a long line of faithful followers*, Paul tells Timothy. *I know that faith lives on in you.* Interestingly enough, Timothy's father was not a believer. Timothy could easily have followed his father into a life of secularism. But instead, he chose the faith of his grandmother and mother. So, too, we must choose the legacy we are going to carry on.

For some, this might mean letting go of a long and difficult past. It might mean choosing forgiveness over bitterness. It might mean leaving an unhealthy relationship, "unfriending" people who do not build us up, or giving up trying to be the perfect wife, daughter, or mother. Choosing a new legacy might mean we have to honestly confront some demons in our past, acknowledging hurt that has been done to us or hurt we have done to others. Choosing a new legacy might mean we have to start telling the truth, scary and painful as it might be.

This week, think about the kind of legacy you are leaving. Are you leaving a legacy of hope or despair? Are you leaving a legacy of love or hate? Are you leaving a legacy of faith for your children and their children, and their children to follow?

Remember the legacy that has been laid before you. God loves you. God sent Christ to die for you. You have salvation. You have hope. You have redemption. You can have restoration. Remember Whose you are. And pass it on.

Dear God, restore my soul. Give me hope. Give me a future. Give me your peace.

Confessions of the Pastor's Wife

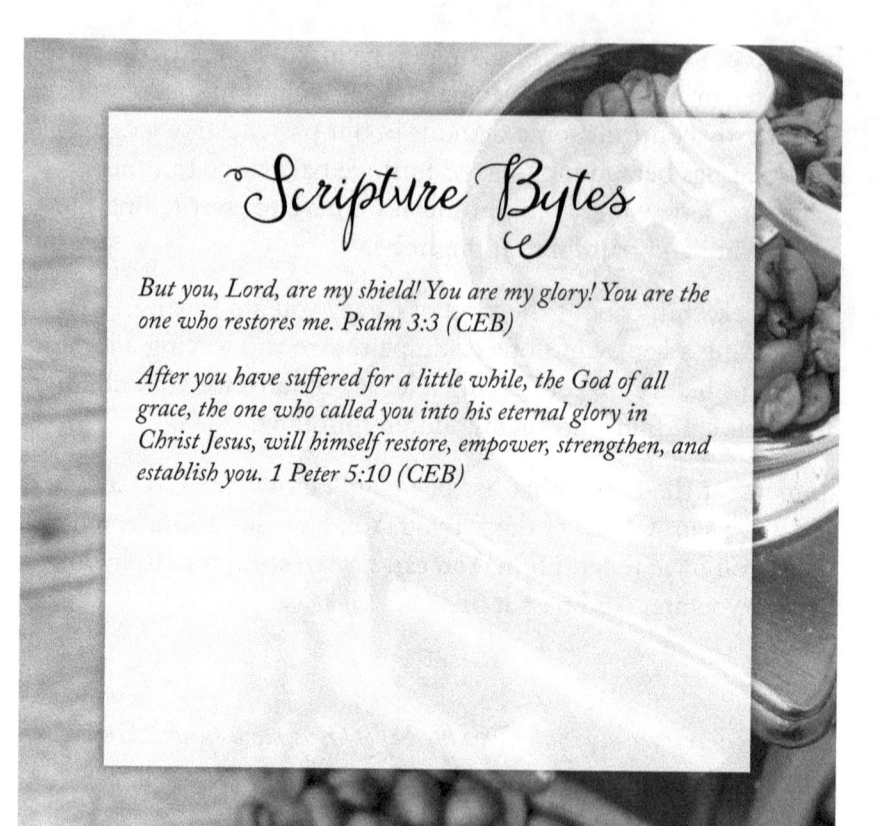

Scripture Bytes

But you, Lord, are my shield! You are my glory! You are the one who restores me. Psalm 3:3 (CEB)

After you have suffered for a little while, the God of all grace, the one who called you into his eternal glory in Christ Jesus, will himself restore, empower, strengthen, and establish you. 1 Peter 5:10 (CEB)

Confessions of the Pastor's Wife

A BIT OF DIRT

When the Pharisee saw that Jesus didn't ritually purify his hands by washing before the meal, he was astonished. The Lord said to him, "Now, you Pharisees clean the outside of the cup and platter, but your insides are stuffed with greed and wickedness. Foolish people! Didn't the one who made the outside also make the inside?"

Luke 11:38-40 (CEB)

I do not, in general, like to get dirty. I don't like to go a day without showering. I don't like it when I'm walking after it rains or snows and dirty water splashes up on my legs from my shoes. I don't buy jeans that look dingy. And I always immediately scrub my hands and fingernails after spending time in the garden. I just don't like dirt.

When my boys were infants, my personal dislike of dirt was transferred to them in that I didn't like them to be dirty either. I didn't like it when their hair started to get flat, or when dirt started to collect under their fingernails. I didn't like it when they spilled food on their clothes, or when they smeared food all over their faces. It wasn't until my boys were toddlers that I realized dirt just naturally comes with them.

I saw this when we spent a day with some good friends who are not opposed to dirt. They have a beautiful old Victorian home with a spacious backyard that flows out from a wide wooden

Confessions of the Pastor's Wife

deck. We gathered on that deck in the warmth of an early summer evening, talking and laughing and watching our children play. The kids ran free in the backyard, playing in a sandbox and with the garden hose. My oldest son, who was one at the time, was crawling around all over the deck.

When night drew on and mosquitos came out, we gathered the kids to go inside and get settled for bed. I noticed that my son was filthy. Not only were his knees dirty, but his shorts, shirt, feet, hands, and face were all smeared with dirt and sweat. My initial instinct was, of course, to give him a bath. But as I looked at his tired face, I realized that he was perfectly content in his state of dirtiness.

The dirt he was covered in meant that he had been doing things, important things. He had been exploring and investigating a brand new world. He had been driving a fire truck and delivering water balloons to a newfound friend. He didn't mind the dirt. It was part of the experience of reveling in the summer evening.

As I lay in bed that night, a thousand similar summer evenings from my own childhood flashed through my mind. I remembered playing outside until sunset, when the street lights came on. I remembered riding bikes through mud puddles and playing in a dusty gravel drive. I remembered using the swimming pool as a big bathtub and going to sleep surrounded by the smell of chlorine mixed with sweat. Those were beautiful days... days of meaning...days of accomplishment.

The truth is, God is much more concerned with our inner state of cleanliness than our outer state of cleanliness. In fact, if we spend too much time focusing on the outside appearance of our lives, we will completely neglect the inner workings of our soul. This is precisely the issue Jesus had with the Pharisees. They were so focused on observing the letter of the law that they forgot the overall purpose of their faith. Jesus reminded them of their purpose by admonishing them and challenging them to give to those in need. Then, Jesus told the Pharisees, you will be clean all over.

Doing the work of Christ in this world means that we are going to get dirty. But like my son, we will be content in the knowledge that our dirt-smeared, sweat-streaked bodies have been doing good and important things—things that bring about the kingdom of God on earth.

This week, think about those things you have been avoiding for fear of getting "dirty." Is there a mission project God is calling you to that would require hard physical labor? Is God asking you to share a message of hope and salvation with those who are imprisoned? Or, are you being led to work with the least of these living out on the streets? Take some time to pray over what God may be asking you to do, remembering that a little dirt is good for the soul.

Loving and Gracious God, glorify the work of your hands, and help me to engage in that work, regardless of how messy it may be.

Confessions of the Pastor's Wife

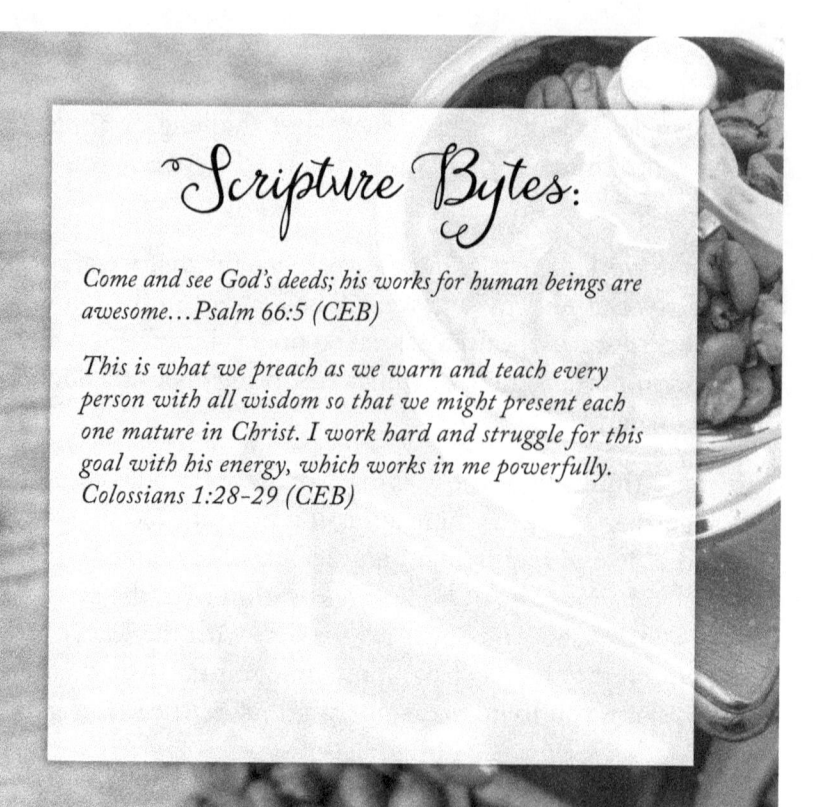

Scripture Bytes:

Come and see God's deeds; his works for human beings are awesome...Psalm 66:5 (CEB)

This is what we preach as we warn and teach every person with all wisdom so that we might present each one mature in Christ. I work hard and struggle for this goal with his energy, which works in me powerfully. Colossians 1:28-29 (CEB)

Confessions of the Pastor's Wife

ROAD CONSTRUCTION

Don't remember the prior things; don't ponder ancient history. Look! I am doing a new thing; now it sprouts up; don't you recognize it? I'm making a way in the desert, paths in the wilderness.

Isaiah 43:18-19 (CEB)

Road construction is always a pain. Several years ago, I commuted to work across a major city whose roads were constantly "under construction." Several major arteries through the city were closed off, and nothing new was opened up to relieve excess traffic. Detours were complicated and poorly labeled and, most frustrating of all, no new progress seemed to be made. In one highly trafficked area, construction had been underway for at least fifteen years. In that fifteen or so years, the highway department worked continuously to build the exact same road structure that was present before, alleviating no traffic problems for the thousands of commuters who went in and out of the city each day. I often wondered, what's the point of all the inconvenience if nothing better is being created?

As a Christian, I often feel like my life is one big road construction area. God has cut off major arteries, sent me on complicated detours, surprised me with unexpected "Road

Confessions of the Pastor's Wife

Closed" signs, and has been working on the same stretch of road for a number of years with no sign of an end in sight. There are times when the road doesn't make sense, and I am frustrated or afraid. Other times, a road ends and I am left alone, feeling sad and like a complete and total failure. But there are also moments of incredible joy and peace—moments where I feel as if I am flying across a straight highway on a beautiful summer day with the windows down and the radio up.

The truth is, there is always a point to the construction in our lives. Although we might not see it right away, God has a plan of action. The work in progress is really a work toward progress. God is not going to spend fifteen, twenty, thirty, or even fifty years rebuilding the same thing. God is always working on rebuilding and renovating to create something better. God says, "Look around! I'm building something new. I'm making a path out of the wilderness of your life. I'm creating streams where there was once only dry parched land. So keep going. I've got a plan."

I don't know where the road of life is taking you right now. Most likely, there is some road construction ahead. When you experience life's detours, dead ends, land closures, and delays, remember that God is not just patching the road. Rather, he is creating something new.

Creator God, you are the Master Architect. Help me to trust in your plans and to follow your blueprint, knowing that there will be detours and construction ahead. Let me press on toward the goal which calls me heavenward in Christ.

Confessions of the Pastor's Wife

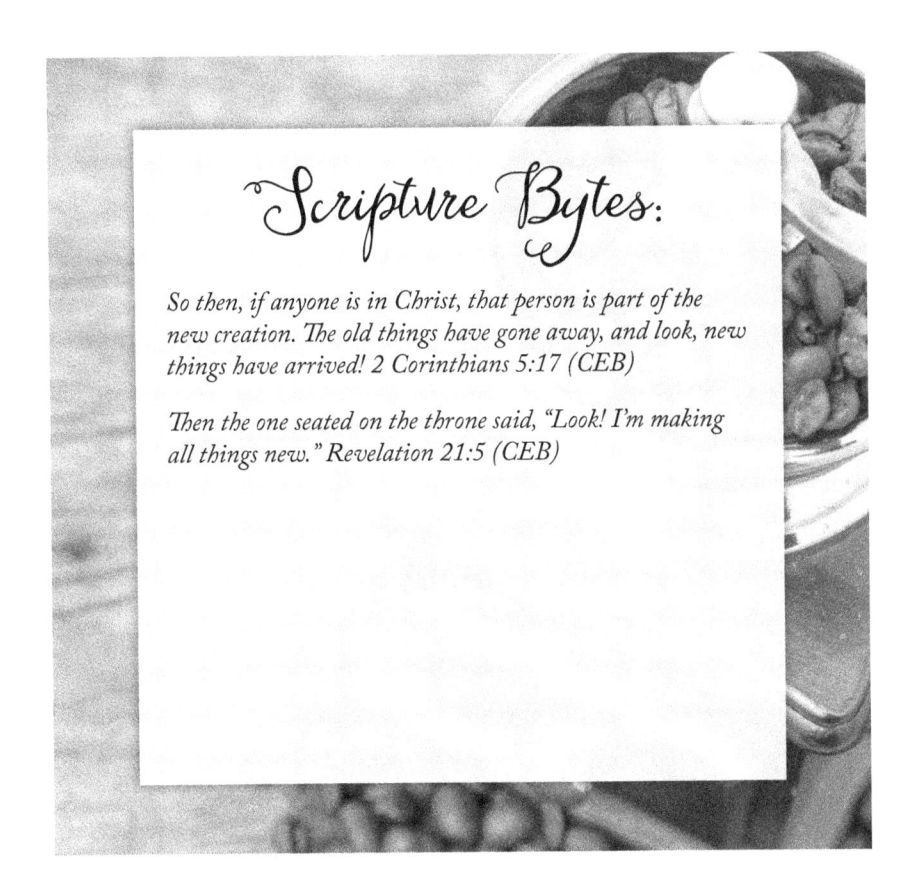

Scripture Bytes:

So then, if anyone is in Christ, that person is part of the new creation. The old things have gone away, and look, new things have arrived! 2 Corinthians 5:17 (CEB)

Then the one seated on the throne said, "Look! I'm making all things new." Revelation 21:5 (CEB)

Confessions of the Pastor's Wife

Confessions of the Pastor's Wife

AN AIR-TIGHT SEAL

I'm convinced that nothing can separate us from God's love in Christ Jesus our Lord: not death or life, not angels or rulers, not present things or future things, not powers or height or depth, or any other thing that is created.

Romans 8:38 (CEB)

One early morning a few years ago, I was putting together a soup for a snack day at school. Everything was prepared so that all I needed to do was plug in the Crock-pot once I got to school. However, as I was pouring the soup into the Crock-pot I realized that I had no idea how I was going to safely get it to the final destination. I was teaching in a town about twenty miles from where I was living and there were several turns, curves, and hills along the way. Staring at the Crock-pot for a minute or so, I had an idea. I pulled the plastic wrap out of a drawer and carefully wrapped it around the lid and top of the cooker. After finishing that, I decided to add an extra layer of protection with aluminum foil. My soup and I successfully made it to school with no spillage.

In thinking about that experience, it occurs to me that this is what God does for our hearts—he takes them and seals them for his own. (Although, probably not with aluminum foil!) When we give our hearts to God, he seals them with his love and grace so that no matter what happens, he is there. God protects and keeps our hearts for him so that with his seal around us, not even the gates of hell will prevail against us. We can stand firm and confident in the knowledge that the Creator of the universe holds us in the palm of his hand!

This doesn't mean, of course, that our lives will be free from sorrow and distress. We live in a human world. People hurt us. Our bodies fail. We make mistakes. There are natural disasters. Accidents happen. Just because God is with us doesn't mean that the tragedies of this world can't touch us. God's seal over our hearts means that these tragedies don't have the final say in our lives. God's seal over our hearts means that in the midst of our darkest moments, God is there. His goodness and strength shine a light into our darkness. His presence gives us hope. The world does not have the final say.

Paul writes in the book of Romans that, "God works all things together for good for the ones who love God, who are called according to his purpose" (Romans 8:28 CEB). This means that when we give our hearts to God, he places his Spirit over them as a seal. This seal is not for safekeeping, but rather, it is a promise—a promise of restoration and redemption. God will protect our hearts so that we can find our hope, our strength, and our peace in him.

Loving God, protector of my soul. You know me. You knit me together in my mother's womb and have numbered the hairs on my head. You know when I'm awake and asleep. You know my thoughts before I can consciously form them. Help me to trust in your safekeeping and care.

Confessions of the Pastor's Wife

Scripture Bytes:

Lord, you have examined me. You know me. You know when I sit down and when I stand up. Even from far away, you comprehend my plans. You study my traveling and resting. You are thoroughly familiar with all my ways. There isn't a word on my tongue, Lord, that you don't already know completely. You surround me—front and back. You put your hand on me. That kind of knowledge is too much for me; it's so high above me that I can't fathom it.

Where could I go to get away from your spirit? Where could I go to escape your presence? If I went up to heaven, you would be there. If I went down to the grave, you would be there too! If I could fly on the wings of dawn, stopping to rest only on the far side of the ocean—even there your hand would guide me; even there your strong hand would hold me tight! If I said, "The darkness will definitely hide me; the light will become night around me," even then the darkness isn't too dark for you! Nighttime would shine bright as day, because darkness is the same as light to you!

Confessions of the Pastor's Wife

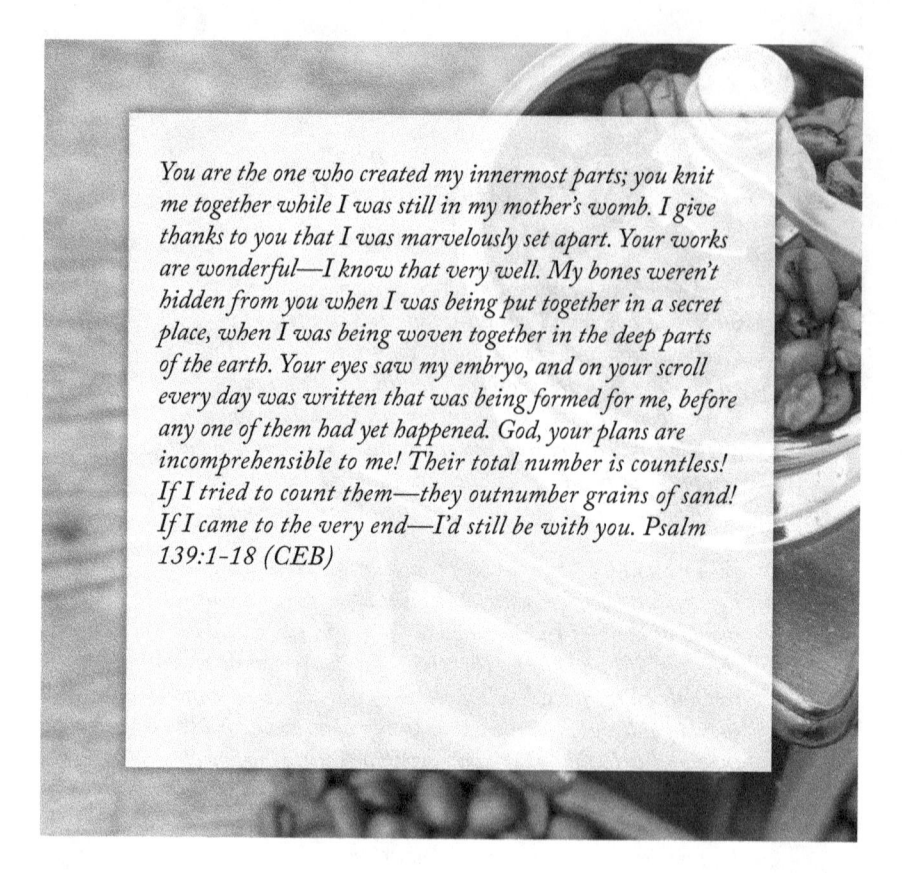

You are the one who created my innermost parts; you knit me together while I was still in my mother's womb. I give thanks to you that I was marvelously set apart. Your works are wonderful—I know that very well. My bones weren't hidden from you when I was being put together in a secret place, when I was being woven together in the deep parts of the earth. Your eyes saw my embryo, and on your scroll every day was written that was being formed for me, before any one of them had yet happened. God, your plans are incomprehensible to me! Their total number is countless! If I tried to count them—they outnumber grains of sand! If I came to the very end—I'd still be with you. Psalm 139:1-18 (CEB)

Confessions of the Pastor's Wife

UNDONE

But after he had considered this, an angel of the Lord appeared to him in a dream and said, "Joseph, son of David, do not be afraid to take Mary home as your wife, because what is conceived in her is from the Holy Spirit. She will give birth to a son, and you are to give him the name Jesus, because he will save his people from their sins."

Matthew 1:20-21 (NIV)

It was twelve days before Christmas, and everything was undone. The tree was up and lit, but only about four ornaments hung from it, haphazardly placed by our boys from early Christmas presents. Neither of our manger scenes were out, as their respective tables were full of random clutter—a fish tank with no fish, twelve jars of peanut butter that were supposed to be taken to the food pantry last summer, a box of play scripts that weren't going to be used until February, books that had popped out of my overflowing bookshelves. There was a basket full of clean laundry in the middle of the living room floor, as well as a plastic tub that formerly housed Christmas tree lights and which my four-year-old was using as his personal gymnastics vault. I don't even think we had gifts purchased, let alone wrapping paper to wrap them in.

Our Advent wreath hung in the closet as its spot on the dining room table was occupied by mail and schoolwork. The Christmas candles were only up because they'd been sitting in place on the top of the china hutch since last December, lost in a layer of dust.

Confessions of the Pastor's Wife

The boys' Christmas tree was sitting on the couch in the living room, the T.V. tray in their room where the tree belonged covered in unhung clothes. And the kitchen had been taken over by grocery bags, newspaper ads, and cups. The whole house had the appearance of being undone.

It occurred to me that undone Christmas, that most of our lives are lived "undone." As Christians, we are constantly waiting in eager expectation for the "consolation of Israel," much like the prophet Simeon in the book of Luke. Our lives are a work in progress, and the final result of all our efforts won't be seen until long after we're gone. Undone is okay.

Don't get me wrong, I would have liked for our house not to look like a federal disaster area for Christmas, but I was perfectly fine with a sparsely ornamented Christmas tree. I had no intention of making a bunch of Christmas treats that no one was going to eat. The kids and I were doing nightly Advent readings without the wreath. And, I knew Baby Jesus would get to his manger whether the fish tank got moved or not.

Undone is what the Christmas story is all about anyway. An unmarried couple was having a baby. Their country was occupied by a hostile foreign force. The baby arrived far away from home. There was no mother, sister, aunt, or cousin around to help with the birth. There wasn't even a room, just a barn. And the first people who came to visit were unclean, uncouth sheep herders. It wasn't quite the perfect moment we work so hard to make our Christmas celebrations out to be.

We spend so much of our time, energy, and money during the month of December trying to get it all just right. In fact, we spend copious amounts of time, energy, and money during the whole year trying to make our lives appear just right. Yet,

Confessions of the Pastor's Wife

God the Creator of heaven and earth came into a world where nothing was right. His people were living under the suffocating oppression of the Roman Empire. His creation was floundering under the devastating power of sin. The world was a mess. The world is still a mess. But God entered into it anyway. God entered into it because it was a mess, and He remains within it today, working through us (and maybe in spite of us) to set things right.

Undone is the place where God dwells. So, if we want to encounter the living, active, moving God, we need to be a little undone too. We need to acknowledge that our lives are a mess and see that mess as an invitation for the Holy One to enter in. God is a creator—he loves undone! So if you're feeling like your life is a bit of a mess at the moment, know that you're in good company. Know, too, that God is there in the midst of it, creating a masterpiece.

Creator God, who formed the world out of nothingness, who came into a messy and broken world in order to redeem it and all who dwell within—enter into my mess. Help me to let go of the idea of perfection, and focus instead on the work you're doing. Help me to see the beauty in the undone spaces, and give me the patience to let you create your masterpiece.

Scripture Bytes:

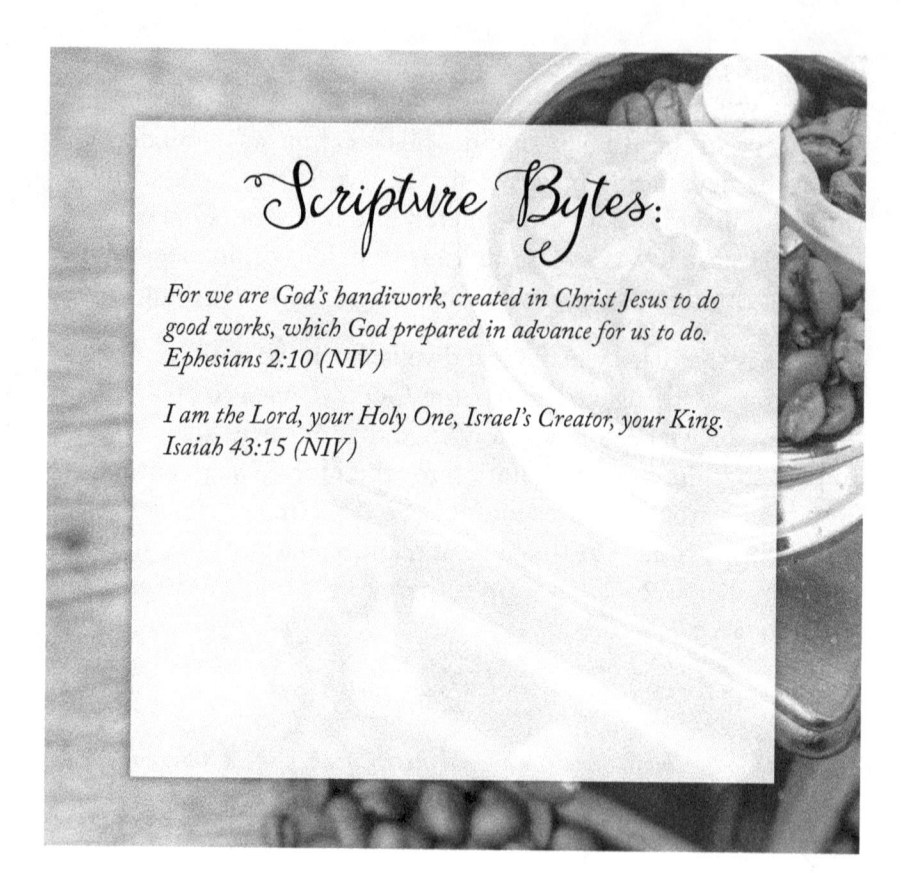

For we are God's handiwork, created in Christ Jesus to do good works, which God prepared in advance for us to do.
Ephesians 2:10 (NIV)

I am the Lord, your Holy One, Israel's Creator, your King.
Isaiah 43:15 (NIV)

Confessions of the Pastor's Wife

Slogging Through the Wilderness

No doubt about it: the Lord your God has blessed you in all that you have done. He watched over your journey through that vast desert. Throughout these forty years, the Lord your God has been with you. You haven't needed a thing.

Deuteronomy 2:7 (CEB)

A few years ago, I decided to take my boys (then ages five and seven), on a short nature hike. It was a hot and humid summer morning, with a forecast of rain later in the day. I carefully studied a trail map before charging down one of the marked paths at the nature center. "We're only going a mile," I promised my skeptical boys. The hike began at a lovely brisk pace. I appreciated the cool shade of the tall oak and maple trees that surrounded us and overhung the bumpy earthen path. We came to a fork in the path and decided to take the tree-lined route. We walked on, and on, and on…

Half an hour later, at the crest of a steep hill, my boys asked, "Where are we?" Mercifully, there was a little wooden bench at

Confessions of the Pastor's Wife

the summit with a beautiful view of woods, woods, and more woods. Taking a deep breath, I confessed, "I don't know."

"We're LOST?" exclaimed my oldest son.

"Well," I countered. "I wouldn't say we're LOST. I mean, we're still on the path in the nature center."

While this was technically true, it was also true that I no longer had any idea which path we were on. Given the distance that we had already covered, I started to suspect that our choice at the fork in the path had led us onto the longer five mile path instead of the one mile I had promised. With nowhere to go but onward, we pushed ahead. Our hike took us beside beautiful, babbling brooks where we encountered turtles, frogs, and fish. At one point we crossed through a field of high, golden grass and saw a snake slithering across our way. Back into the shade of the woods, the skies opened and the rain began to pour. Finally, exhausted and wet, we saw the dark roof of the visitor's center in the distance. A few hills and several turns later, we were back where we began.

Since our "little" nature hike, my boys have absolutely refused to take any wooded path with me again. I had promised them a light and carefree romp through the forest. Instead, we ended up slogging through the wilderness for over two hours.

It occurred to me that this, indeed, is how my life sometimes feels. Instead of the invigorating walk I expect, I find myself stumbling around a vast wilderness. When I want a clear and direct route, God seems more inclined to lead me through overgrown, unmarked forest paths that intertwine and wrap around and cross over mud-bottomed streams full of catfish (which I don't even like to eat). It's irritating. And as much as I whine and complain, God continues to stand resolute, arms

Confessions of the Pastor's Wife

crossed over his expansive chest saying, "You're just gonna have to keep slogging through, baby."

You see, one of the things I believe is that God is much more interested in the "what" of who we are than the "where." God wants to make sure our life journey leads us closer and closer to him. Therefore, he's willing to let us slog it out in muddy streams and overgrown paths in order to complete the great and perfect work in us He has begun. And not only is God willing to let us slog it out, he will patiently stand before us and wait while we dig our heels into the muddy bank and get our full stubborn on.

However, God knows that regardless of how long we choose to sit on that muddy shore in a pout, we will eventually pull ourselves up and slog on through. And we will do this because no matter how crazy and complicated and irritating the path seems, we believe that God will get us back home in the end.

God sees the bigger, eternal picture of things. He is working right now not only on our future, but on the future of our children and grandchildren and great-grandchildren. There are things coming together right now that we will never see—things that we cannot comprehend or know but that will matter someday down the line of legacy.

While my boys did not appreciate their five mile cross-country hike in the moment, it is something they still look back on and remember quite vividly. I have to think that, someday, the memory of that trek will sustain them in their own wilderness journeys—that they will remember the joy and elation of reaching their destination, and feel a sense of accomplishment for making it through the arduous path.

Confessions of the Pastor's Wife

I pray, also, that you and I will have the faith to keep on slogging through our own wilderness journeys—that we will experience joy and elation when we finally reach our destination—and that we will discover God's strength that he has so graciously placed within us.

Dear God, guide my paths. Stay near to me, even through the densest part of the wilderness. Although I may not see where the path leads, help me to trust in you. Grant me your strength to keep slogging through, and let me experience the joy of reaching your destination.

Scripture Bytes:

God led his own people out like sheep, guiding them like a flock in the wilderness. Psalm 78:52 (CEB)

Now may our God and Father himself and our Lord Jesus guide us on our way back to you. 1 Thessalonians 3:11 (CEB)

Confessions of the Pastor's Wife

MISSING THE MARK BY AN INCH

If I did want to brag, I wouldn't make a fool of myself because I'd tell the truth. I'm holding back from bragging so that no one will give me any more credit than what anyone sees or hears about me. I was given a thorn in my body because of the outstanding revelations I've received so that I wouldn't be conceited. It's a messenger from Satan sent to torment me so that I wouldn't be conceited. I pleaded with the Lord three times for it to leave me alone. He said to me, "My grace is enough for you, because power is made perfect in weakness." So I'll gladly spend my time bragging about my weaknesses so that Christ's power can rest on me.

2 Corinthians 12:6-9 (CEB)

One hundred eleven pitches. That was the pitch count for a rookie pitcher in a professional baseball game my husband and I were watching. One hundred eleven pitches in the top of the ninth inning with no hits against him. One hundred eleven pitches and two outs. One hundred eleven pitches and one out away from becoming only the twelfth pitcher in our favorite franchise's history to pitch a no hitter. And then came pitch 112.

Confessions of the Pastor's Wife

As the young pitcher released the throw the ball soared smack into the bat of the opposing hitter. Pitch 112 soared over the head of the head of the pitcher, his glove grazing the ball as he stretched his arm, trying to stop the ball from hitting the ground. But, to no avail. Pitch 112 was a hit. The no-hitter was missed by no more than an inch. One hundred twelve pitches. What a difference one pitch makes!!

It's kind of like that in life sometimes, isn't it? Everything seems to be coming together, dreams seem an inch within reach. And then, there's pitch 112. The promotion you were sure of went to someone else. The contract on your dream house falls through. You get yet another rejection letter. You find yourself throwing up in the bathroom behind the sanctuary on Christmas Eve. Oh wait, that's only in my family!

The point is, life happens. Plans go awry. And it can hurt—a lot. Kind of like a thorn in your side. And like Paul, in those moments when it all seems to fall apart, we need to remember that God's grace is enough. Our failures and mistakes and disappointments are okay. In fact, they're perfect. They're an opportunity for God to step in and show his glory and majesty. They're an opportunity for God to show his strength and for us to experience his love in a magnificently remarkable way. God shines on pitch 112.

God shines because we miss it. When Paul brags about his weaknesses, it's not a competition to see whose life is the biggest mess. In fact, Paul is not really bragging about his weakness at all; rather, he's bragging on God. Paul recognizes that all he has accomplished is because of God. Paul's bragging is an acknowledgement that without God, he would be nothing. Where others saw failure and flaws, Paul saw an opportunity to experience the divine presence.

Confessions of the Pastor's Wife

Perhaps you have been feeling like you've missed the mark recently. You've suffered a rejection, you've missed an opportunity, plans have gone awry. Instead of looking at these situations as failures, invite God into them. View them as an opportunity to experience God's presence in a new and powerful way. Rest assured that God is there, God is working, God will provide.

For the record, the young pitcher didn't view pitch 112 as a failure. With a shrug and a big smile, he said, "I guess it just wasn't meant to be." For him, eight and two/thirds innings of no hits was a great game.

Dear God, help me to accept my failures and weaknesses. Let me see them as an opportunity to experience you in a new and powerful way. Work in the midst of my mistakes, missed opportunities, and rejections. Help me, like Paul, to brag on you.

Scripture Bytes:

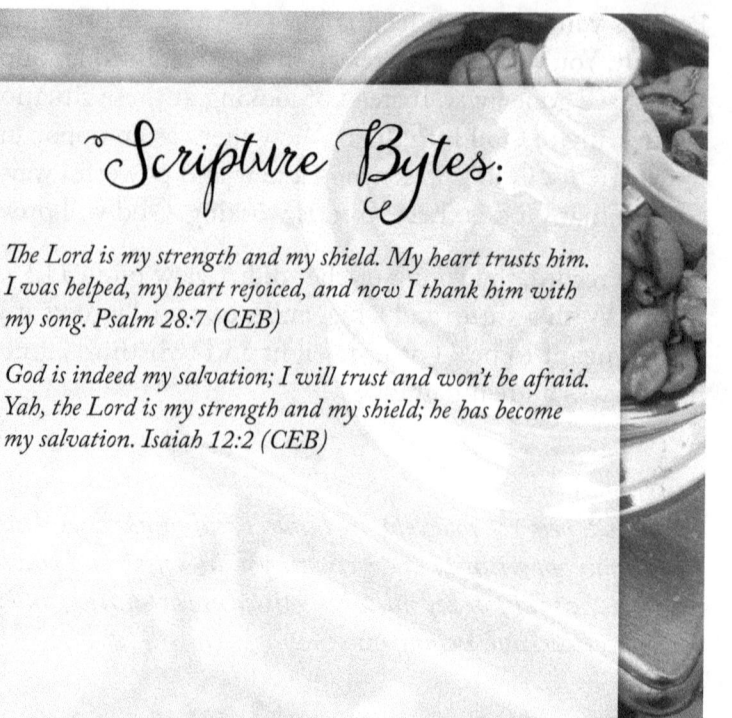

The Lord is my strength and my shield. My heart trusts him. I was helped, my heart rejoiced, and now I thank him with my song. Psalm 28:7 (CEB)

God is indeed my salvation; I will trust and won't be afraid. Yah, the Lord is my strength and my shield; he has become my salvation. Isaiah 12:2 (CEB)

Confessions of the Pastor's Wife

ASK FOR HELP

But Ruth replied, "Don't urge me to leave you or to turn back from you. Where you go I will go, and where you stay I will stay. Your people will be my people and your God my God. Where you die I will die, and there I will be buried. May the Lord deal with me, be it ever so severely, if even death separates you and me." When Naomi realized that Ruth was determined to go with her, she stopped urging her.

Ruth 1:16-18 (NIV)

"When was the last time you asked someone for help?"

As I asked this question to a group of women gathered around our dining room table for Bible study, the resounding response was…silence. None of us could think of a time in recent memory when we had asked another person for help. Chances are, you can't recall the last time you asked someone for help, either. Most of us, if we're being honest, prefer to give help rather than receive it.

Independence is a highly valued concept in our society. It might even rest in the fabric of our subconscious. We want freedom. We want to do our own thing. Thousands upon thousands of self-help books line bookshelves across the country. Do-it-yourself home improvement shows have increased in popularity. Individual athletes are hailed for their talent and make more money than anyone else on their team. And social media encourages us to present to the public lives that are fun, busy, and "happy." Asking for help would admit to the world that, sometimes, our lives are not as perfect as they seem.

Sometimes, in our crazy, frenetic, stress-filled lives, we need a little extra support.

As a pastor's wife, I sometimes fall into the ridiculous assumption that I have to appear to have it all together. My role is to help others. Therefore, I need to be positive, upbeat, and focused on the needs of those around me rather than trolling out my own struggles and grief. While ministering to others is important, I'm not a robot. My life isn't perfect. Like everyone else, some days are better than others.

A good friend of mine called me out on this a few years ago. We were emailing back and forth and most of my emails consisted of things like, "We're fine. The boys are good. Church is great. Let's talk about you." Fed up with generic emails, she finally replied, "You know, you don't have to be a pastor's wife around me." A light bulb went off in my head. While choosing to remain positive and upbeat is important, it's also important to be authentic. And the truth is that sometimes, even I need a little extra support!

God never meant for our lives to be lived in solitary confinement. God recognized the importance of human support in his creation of Eve to be a partner to Adam. Jesus sent the disciples out in pairs to minister to others, and Paul always had at least one travelling companion. We need others because we need support in our lives. God works through the encouragement, advice, understanding, wisdom, and helping hands of others. Not only should we be all of those things for others, *we need to acknowledge our need for them in our own lives.*

Confessions of the Pastor's Wife

Asking for help isn't a bad thing, it's actually the way we were designed. God doesn't want us to be able to do it all on our own! Rather, God wants us to need some help—he wants us to be dependent on him! In order to depend on God, we have to sometimes depend on others. *We need support.* And it's a good thing. There's a mutuality in support. While Ruth supported Naomi, Naomi also worked to support Ruth. They depended on one another. And they both depended on God.

So ask for help. It's okay. God, in his perfect wisdom and understanding has already provided just what you need.

Loving and Gracious God, thank you for giving me the people in my life who support me. Thank you for providing me friends and family to depend on in times of need. Help me to have the courage to ask for help, to graciously receive help that is offered, and to extend the hand of support to others.

Scripture Bytes:

...the Lord commissioned seventy-two others and sent them on ahead in pairs to every city and place he was about to go. Luke 10:1 (CEB)

They are known as the residents of the holy city, those who depend on the God of Israel...Isaiah 48:2 (CEB)

Confessions of the Pastor's Wife

TACO TUESDAYS

Bless the God and Father of our Lord Jesus Christ! He has blessed us in Christ with every spiritual blessing that comes from heaven.

Ephesians 1:3 (CEB)

When we lived in Kansas City, one of our weekly rituals was to go to "Taco Tuesday" at one of our two favorite local Mexican joints. "Taco Tuesday" is an all-you-can-eat, buy-one-get-one-free, homemade beef taco extravaganza. Although it's been a couple of years since I've indulged in one, I can still taste the crispy fried goodness as the meat, cheese, and corn tortilla all melted together in my mouth.

Although the tacos were good, I don't think they are the reason the memory of "Taco Tuesdays" invokes such a deep sense of fulfillment and peace in my soul. Rather, it's the memories of those who gathered with us on those Tuesdays that I cherish. It was sacred time among family and friends.

More often than not, we would meet my sister and her husband for taco dinner. The wait time was always fairly lengthy, so we had lots of opportunity to chat and laugh and vent about our day. Other times, we would head out with my husband's co-workers for a semi-quick lunch. Out of the church office, we could more freely share together the joys and struggles of professional ministry.

Confessions of the Pastor's Wife

"Taco Tuesdays" became a little sacred ritual in our lives. And, as I think back on it, I realize what a blessing those small "everyday" rituals can be. They give us the opportunity to stop, reflect, share, dream, laugh, fill-up, relax, and engage with those who matter the most to us. It's in these "everyday" rituals that we are free to be the people God created us to be, that we get a sense of ourselves within our community of family and friends, that we develop the supports we need to continue doing the work God has called us to do.

It's important to note that most of our "everyday" rituals seem to be born from spontaneity. "Taco Tuesdays" started out because someone said, "Hey, let's go get some tacos." The sacredness evolved with time and repetition.

I could give example after example of "everyday" rituals that have been sacred time in my life. But my guess is, you're already reflecting on your own spaces and places of "everyday" sacred experiences. I would love for you to claim them and name them, to give thanks for the wonderful blessings these "everyday" rituals provide.

Dear God, thank you for the blessings of the everyday moments. Help me to seek out sacred moments for my family, time that we can cherish one another and draw closer to you.

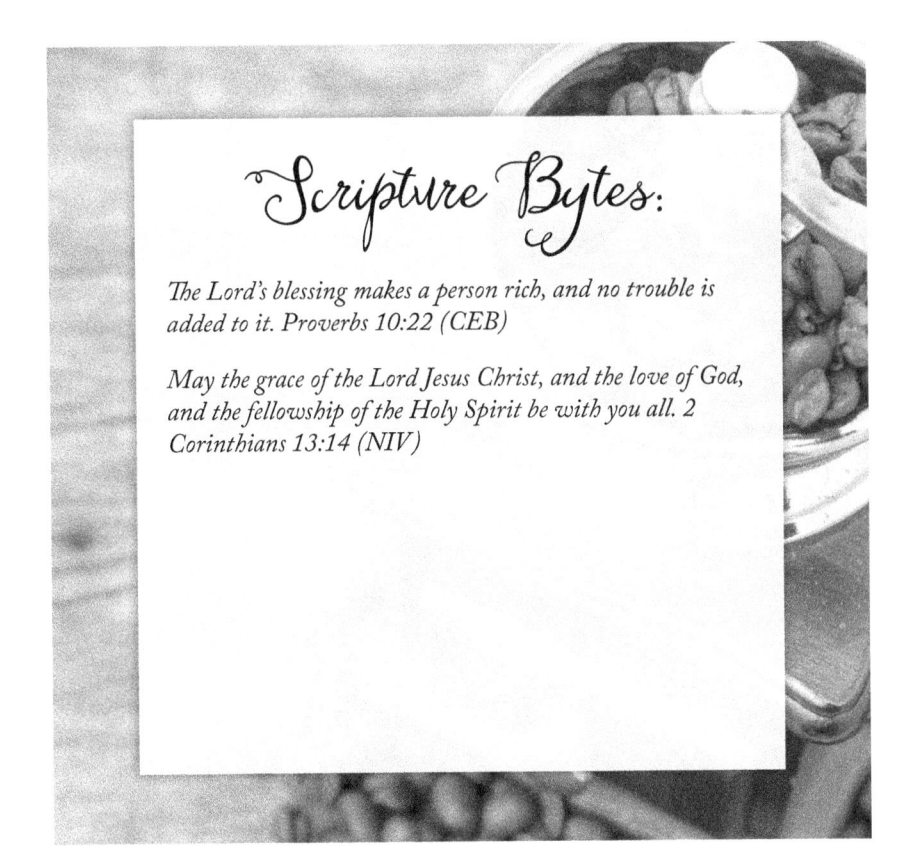

Scripture Bytes:

The Lord's blessing makes a person rich, and no trouble is added to it. Proverbs 10:22 (CEB)

May the grace of the Lord Jesus Christ, and the love of God, and the fellowship of the Holy Spirit be with you all. 2 Corinthians 13:14 (NIV)

Confessions of the Pastor's Wife

Confessions of the Pastor's Wife

ACCEPTING GOD'S CALL

We are the ones God has called…

Romans 9:24 (CEB)

When God calls us to a task, it is rarely ever an easy thing to do. Oftentimes, the work seems impossible. Always, the task at hand is one that takes time, trust, and infinite patience. We don't feel qualified, prepared, worthy, or even desirous of the opportunity God is presenting. In reality, we're probably not qualified, prepared, or worthy of the opportunity.

Listen to some of the responses of people in Scripture who have been called by God:

> **Moses:** I have never been a good speaker. I wasn't one before you spoke to me, and I'm not one now. I am slow at speaking, and I can never think of what to say. (Exodus 4:10 CEV)

> **Esther:** There is a law about going in to see the king, and all his officials and his people know about this law. Anyone who goes into see the king without being invited by him will be put to death. (Esther 4:11 CEV)

Confessions of the Pastor's Wife

>**Gideon:** Please don't take this wrong, but if the Lord is helping us, then why have all these awful things happened? (Judges 6:13 CEV)
>
>**Jeremiah:** I'm not a good speaker Lord, and I'm too young. (Jeremiah 1:6 CEV)
>
>**Zechariah:** My wife and I are both very old. (Luke 1:18 CEV)
>
>**Mary:** How can this happen? I am not married! (Luke 1:34) (CEV)
>
>**Ananias:** Lord, a lot of people have told me about the terrible things this man has done. (Acts 9:13) (CEV)

Do any of these objections to a call sound familiar to you? I'm too old. I'm too young. I've never done this before. I'm not in the right season of my life. I don't have enough experience in this field. It's too dangerous. I don't trust you. You're asking too much.

If we're being honest with ourselves, we've used a couple of these objections with God once or twice before. I have used the "this isn't a good season in my life" objection way too frequently. I mean, how much can God expect me to do with two small children in tow? (A lot!)

You see, God knows what our objections are going to be before we ever voice them. And God not only hears our objections, He prepares and blows them out of the water.

Listen to God's reply to His faithful servants:

>**To Moses:** Who makes people able to speak or makes them deaf or unable to speak? Who gives them sight or makes them blind? Don't you know that I am the one who does these things? Now go! When you speak, I will be with you and give

you the words to say. (Oh, and take your brother-in-law Aaron. He's a great public speaker!) (Exodus 4:11-12) (CEV)

To Esther via Mordecai: Don't think that you will escape being killed with the rest of the Jews, just because you live in the king's palace. If you don't speak up now, we will somehow get help, but you and your family will be killed. It could be that you were made queen for a time like this! (Esther 4:13-14) (CEV)

To Gideon: Gideon, you will be strong, because I am giving you the power to rescue Israel from the Midianites. (Judges 6:14) (CEV)

To Jeremiah: Don't say you're too young. If I tell you to go and speak to someone, then go! And when I tell you what to say, don't leave out a word! I promise to be with you and keep you safe, so don't be afraid. (Jeremiah 1:7-8) (CEV)

To Zechariah via Gabriel: You have not believed what I have said. So you will not be able to say a thing until all this happens. But everything will take place when it is supposed to. (Luke 1:20) (CEV)

To Mary via Gabriel: The Holy Spirit will come down to you, and God's power will come over you. Nothing is impossible for God! (Luke 1:35-37) (CEV)

To Ananias: Go! I have chosen him to tell foreigners, kings, and the people of Israel about me. (Acts 9:15) (CEV)

You see, God doesn't care if we're old, or young, or single or married, or experienced, or well-trained, or prepared or have young children. Each and every time we raise an objection, God says, "GO! I AM is going to take care of everything you need!"

Confessions of the Pastor's Wife

God doesn't need us to be anything but obedient, because HE is everything else. When God calls us to a task, He makes a sacred promise to be with us throughout the entire completion of the project. God knows we can't do it on our own—that's actually part of the point. We can't. God can. We go. God does. And then, God is glorified and magnified and we have experienced the love of God in deep and profound new ways.

The apostle Paul writes that Christ's power is made stronger when we are weak. When we face a task for which we know we are not qualified, trained, or are scared to do, then we have to turn ourselves completely over to God. And that is what God desires most of all—His children depending and relying on Him. And when we give ourselves fully and completely over to God, amazing things can happen.

Call to me, Lord, for I am your servant. I am listening for you. Send me forth to do your will. Equip me for the task, and let my work honor you.

Scripture Bytes:

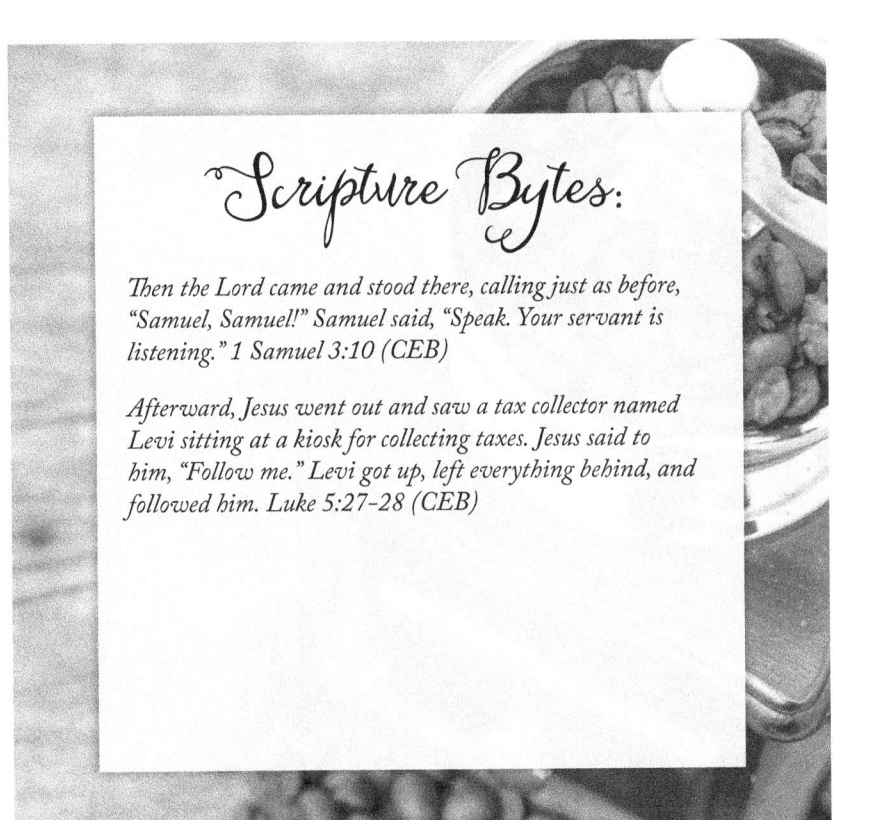

Then the Lord came and stood there, calling just as before, "Samuel, Samuel!" Samuel said, "Speak. Your servant is listening." 1 Samuel 3:10 (CEB)

Afterward, Jesus went out and saw a tax collector named Levi sitting at a kiosk for collecting taxes. Jesus said to him, "Follow me." Levi got up, left everything behind, and followed him. Luke 5:27-28 (CEB)

Confessions of the Pastor's Wife

HEARING GOD'S CALL

Samuel said, "Speak. Your servant is listening."

1 Samuel 3:10 (CEB)

I have often dreamed of walking outside and finding our front shrubbery on fire—partly because I don't like shrubbery, and partly because I think it would be an announcement I couldn't easily miss. If God sets fire to your hedge and then speaks to you from within it, you're probably going to notice!

Yet more often than not, God chooses to reveal himself quietly, through the natural ebb and flow of my daily life. God speaks to me through his Word, while listening to praise songs, in a conversation with a friend, or in the stirring of my heart through worship.

God speaks in the "still, small voice" Elijah hears in the cave after the fire, wind and earthquake have passed. (1 Kings 19:10-14).

And it's easy to miss.

Look at young Samuel's call story:

> *The Lord called out Samuel's name. Samuel ran to Eli and said, "Here I am. What do you want?"*

Confessions of the Pastor's Wife

"I didn't call you," Eli answered. "Go back to bed."

Samuel went back.

Again the Lord called out Samuel's name. Samuel got up and went to Eli. "Here I am," he said. "What do you want?"

Eli told him, "Son, I didn't call you. Go back to sleep."

The Lord had not spoken to Samuel before, and Samuel did not recognize the voice. When the Lord called out his name for the third time, Samuel went to Eli again and said, "Here I am. What do you want?"

Eli finally realized that it was the Lord who was speaking to Samuel. So he said, "Go back and lie down! If someone speaks to you again, answer, 'I'm listening, Lord. What do you want me to do?'"

1 Samuel 3:4-9 (CEV)

I love this story of Samuel's calling. I think it speaks so much to the quiet and subtle ways in which God calls us and our ability (or inability) to discern his voice.

In this passage, Samuel is living in the house of the Lord. He is sleeping just feet from the altar. His life is dedicated to the Lord's service, and he is absolutely ready to serve. He is so eager to prove himself that he runs to Eli in the middle of the night prepared for whatever task he believes Eli is calling him to perform.

Samuel eagerly wanted to serve. He lived in anticipation of purpose.

I've found that within most of us dwells a deep desire to be of service. We want to help others. We want to fight for a noble cause. We are eager to have a purpose. But, like Samuel, we can get confused about whom we are to serve.

Confessions of the Pastor's Wife

We get caught up in the demands of our careers, our outside activities, our families, and our hobbies. We get so involved in being busy that we cannot identify the voice of the One calling to us. Instead of stopping and listening, really listening, we work harder, add on new projects, and exhaust ourselves trying to chase after something that has been standing before us the entire time.

God was right in front of Samuel, but Samuel couldn't recognize him. Samuel lived and worked in the House of the Lord, but he had no recognition of God's voice. Samuel spent his childhood working for God, but he never took the time to *know* God. Thankfully, Samuel had a trusted spiritual advisor who could help him learn.

Thankfully for us, God sends those advisors our way too. Sometimes our spouses, parents, siblings, friends, and co-workers can see God calling to us when we can't. This is one of the reasons why it is so important to have strong, spiritually-deep people in our lives and why it's important to cultivate our own deep spiritual roots. Who knows but that you could be someone else's Eli?

The key is we have to be willing to *listen*. And part of *listening* is knowing just exactly WHOM we are listening to. I can't tell you if God is calling you to something or not. God speaks to each of us in his own way and in his own time. I hear God speak to me as I read his Word. I hear him as he places his thoughts in my mind during times of prayer.

Others hear him speak through music and worship. Some hear him speak through teachers, pastors, and spiritual leaders. For others, God comes with great and dramatic bush-burning flair. There's no rhyme, although there's always a reason.

Confessions of the Pastor's Wife

So *listen* for God as he seeks to speak with you today.

Be still and *listen*.

God of all wisdom, power, and strength, don't let me miss a word from you. Give me ears that I might hear, eyes that I may see, and a mind that I might understand. Speak, Lord, for your servant is listening.

Scripture Bytes:

After the fire, there was a sound. Thin. Quiet. When Elijah heard it, he wrapped his face in his coat. He went out and stood at the cave's entrance. A voice came to him and said, "Why are you here, Elijah?" 1 Kings 19:12-13 (CEB)

My sheep listen to my voice. I know them and they follow me. John 10:27 (CEB)

Confessions of the Pastor's Wife

WONDER MOMENTS

Thank God for His gift that is too wonderful for words!

2 Corinthians 9:15 (CEV)

I leaned back on the bathmat, watching my boys splash, laugh, and play in the water. I looked at their faces, so bright and happy, and full of innocence, hope, and possibility. I smiled, drinking in the moment when I didn't have anywhere else to be or anything else to do. I could focus my entire attention on these two precious gifts God had given me. And it hit me there in that bathroom, on a typical Wednesday night—this is a sacred moment. This is a wonder moment.

As a parent of young children, most of my time is spent just making it through the day. I get up, get ready, get the kids ready, get lunches ready, drive to work, work, drive home, get kids home, monitor homework, attempt a conversation with my husband, get kids ready for bed, get kids to bed, unwind, get myself to bed, and do it all over again the next day.

I'm not complaining. It's a good life, one I am incredibly grateful to have. But I have to admit, I don't always appreciate moments with my children for the wonderful gifts they are. Often, I send

Confessions of the Pastor's Wife

them out to play, or to color, or to watch TV while I work on something else. I get their hair washed in the bath and run out to do a load of laundry or catch up on e-mail.

Fortunately, God has infinitely more wisdom than me!

There are times when he breaks through the everyday plodding and reminds me that this time, frantic and chaotic as it may be, is sacred. God gives me those wonder moments when I remember what is truly important and can let go of the mundane to feast on the extraordinary. And the truly extraordinary is the time spent fully attuned to and connected with my family.

There are sacred elements that each day holds, if only we can turn our focus onto them. Maybe it's that moment right before you wake your children from their sleep, when you look down at the innocence and beauty of their faces. Perhaps it's the evening sunset you share with a friend while walking down a path, sharing and supporting one another along the journey. Maybe it's the cup of coffee you share with your spouse, drinking in the goodness of quiet moments spent together before rushing into the day.

How much more content would we be in our lives if we practiced the art of recognizing the sacred moments within them? Could something as mundane as washing dishes become a wonder moment if we truly stopped to appreciate the beauty of clean water and turned our thoughts to the One who created it?

This week, consider what wonder moments could God have in store for you if you would see them. Then, offer up a prayer of thanksgiving for the beauty of your daily life.

Confessions of the Pastor's Wife

Creator God, thank you for creating the wonder moments in my life. Help me to see the sacredness of even the most mundane tasks. Help me to pause and appreciate the beauty of your blessings all around me.

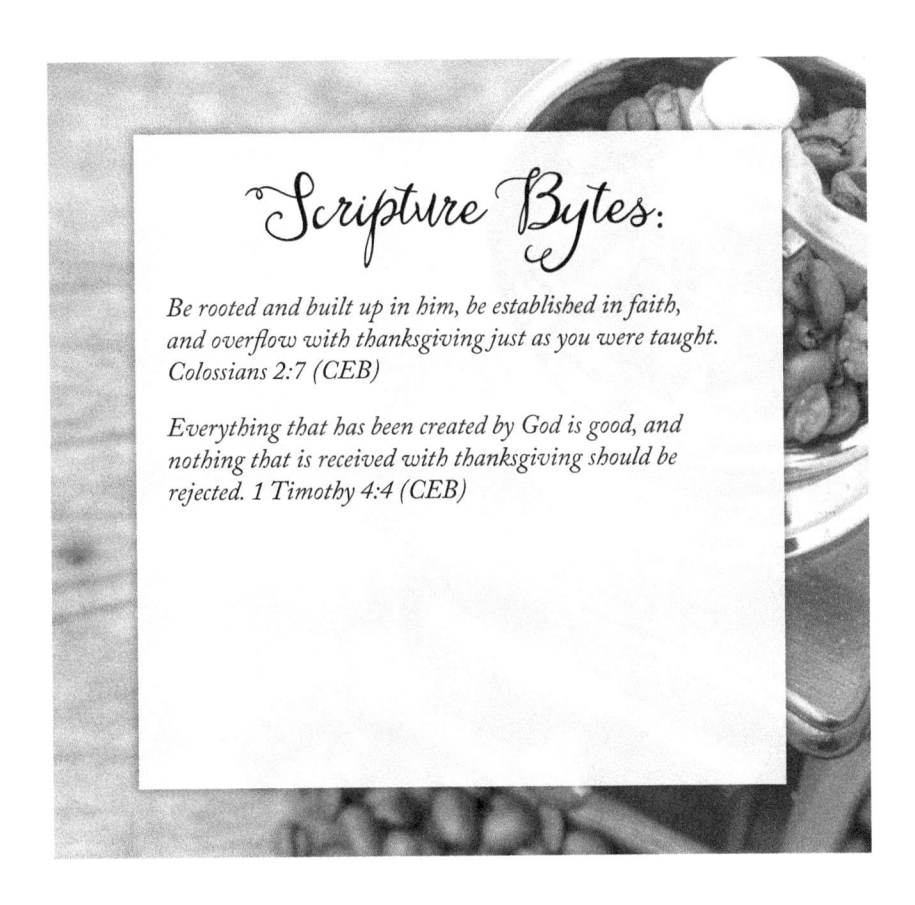

Scripture Bytes:

Be rooted and built up in him, be established in faith, and overflow with thanksgiving just as you were taught. Colossians 2:7 (CEB)

Everything that has been created by God is good, and nothing that is received with thanksgiving should be rejected. 1 Timothy 4:4 (CEB)

Confessions of the Pastor's Wife

Confessions of the Pastor's Wife

THE NATURE OF GRATITUDE

I prayed for this boy, and the Lord gave me what I asked from him. So now I give this boy back to the Lord. As long as he lives, he is given to the Lord.

1 Samuel 1:27-28 (CEB)

One morning, I was giving my oldest son his daily cup of apple juice. In between gulps, he offered a muffled, "Thanks." While I appreciated the politeness, I suddenly realized that his politeness wasn't actually gratitude.

Gratitude is a difficult concept. At its core, gratitude is our physical response to something we greatly appreciate. It is a "return of kindness." There is a big difference between giving thanks and showing gratitude. Thanks is easy. It's rote. Someone opens a door for you and you say, "Thank you." You don't even have to make eye contact.

I think most of us can come up with a list of things we are thankful for. I'm guessing if I asked you, yours would look a lot like mine. I'm thankful for my husband, my children, my family, and my friends. I'm thankful for a job, for a house, for food, and for transportation. I can say, "Thanks." However, I don't always show gratitude. I don't always look at my life and say to God, "You have given me more than enough." I don't often let gratitude fuel my actions.

The difference between giving thanks and showing gratitude is in the application of the sentiments. While thanks is something we say, gratitude is something we do. It is an action of appreciation we take when we are truly grateful for the blessings in our lives. It is our "cup running over and pouring out" love to someone else.

Gratitude is what Hannah showed when she took her most treasured gift, her only son, to the Tabernacle and gave him to God. This child, Samuel, was the only thing Hannah had ever wanted. Can you imagine the joy that filled her soul the day he was born? Can you imagine how cherished he was? How loved he was? She could have said, "Thanks," and moved on. But instead, she chose to give something out of the fullness of her heart. In gratitude, she handed Samuel over to Eli the priest, to be raised in service to the Lord. She gave back to God what God had so graciously given to her. And what amazing plans God had in store for Samuel!

Hannah's gratitude is a reminder to us of the need to show gratitude in our lives. We need to act in ways that demonstrate our love and appreciation for those family and friends God has placed in our lives. Maybe that means playing more with your children, or going to a ballgame with your spouse. Perhaps you need to call your parents more (just because), or take a special friend out to coffee.

Showing gratitude means that we need to take the resources God has given us and use them to benefit others. This isn't just about how we spend our money. It also involves our time, our gifts, our talents, and our strengths.

Confessions of the Pastor's Wife

Showing gratitude means slowing down and enjoying what we already have. We need to take our "more than enough" gifts and give them back to God for use in his service.

Gratitude is hard. It puts others first. It goes against the grain of our culture. But I think, if we can get it, if we can show it, then our lives are going to be a little more fulfilled.

God, thank you for the abundance of gifts in my life. Thank you for family, for friends, for the daily provisions I take for granted. Help me to live a life of gratitude. Let my words and actions show others how truly grateful I am.

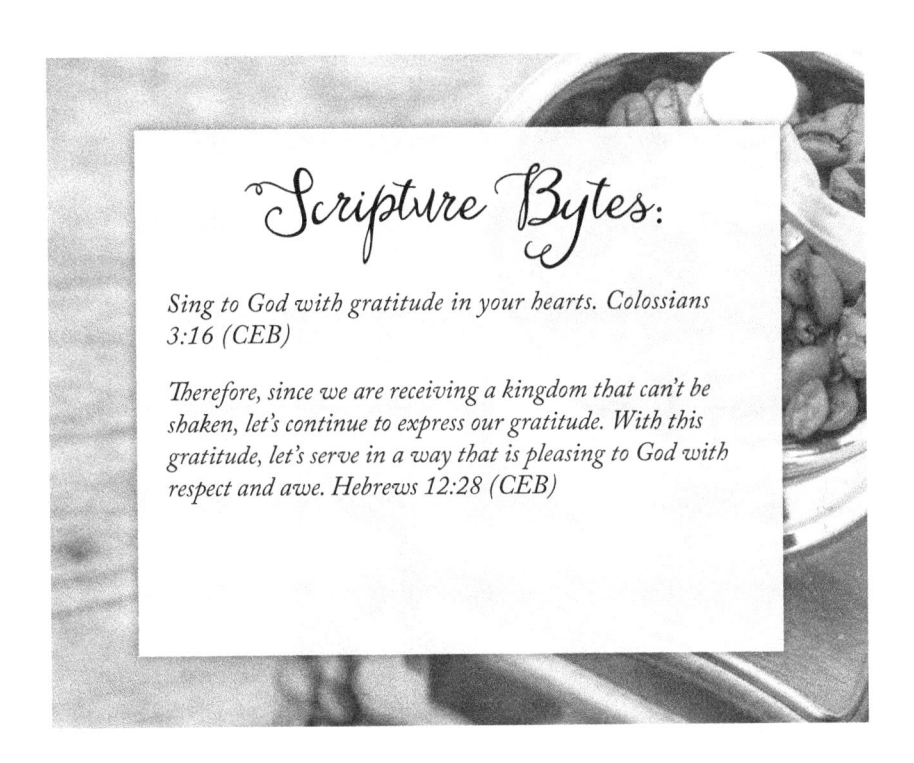

Scripture Bytes:

Sing to God with gratitude in your hearts. Colossians 3:16 (CEB)

Therefore, since we are receiving a kingdom that can't be shaken, let's continue to express our gratitude. With this gratitude, let's serve in a way that is pleasing to God with respect and awe. Hebrews 12:28 (CEB)

Confessions of the Pastor's Wife

Confessions of the Pastor's Wife

BEING A FAITH WARRIOR

Together (we) will be like mighty warriors in battle trampling (our) enemy into the mud of the streets. (We) will fight because the Lord is with (us), and (we) will put the enemy's horsemen to shame.

Zechariah 10:5 (NIV)

Growing up, my Grandpa always told me I would make a good soldier. Why, I have no idea, but it's something he told me over and over. And while I am stubborn, persistent, and more inclined to fight than flee, I don't like being told what to do, I need to know the reason for doing something before I begin, and if someone is pointing a gun in my general direction, I am going to run the other way! I've never seen myself as a warrior. And yet, in the above Scripture, that is precisely what we are called to be!

One look at our society and it becomes clear that we are indeed mighty warriors in battle. The enemy surrounds us, and his weapons are powerful and destructive, breaking us down from within through fear, despair, self-loathing, hopelessness, temptation, guilt, anger, selfishness, materialism, and pride. But we, as followers of Christ, have something even more powerful than these weapons of mass destruction. The Lord is with us!

Confessions of the Pastor's Wife

And he carries in his arsenal not weapons with which to destroy, but tools with which to build.

The Lord brings hope, salvation, grace, mercy, forgiveness, redemption, restoration, healing, peace, goodness, power, strength, faith, compassion perseverance, and love.

As followers of Christ, we will put the enemy to shame with these tools the Lord provides.

We will put the enemy to shame when we choose to forgive rather than hold a grudge.

We will put the enemy to shame when we offer a place of healing in our churches to those who have suffered from addiction.

We will put the enemy to shame when we go out to serve others with love and compassion in the face of despair, disaster, and poverty.

We will put the enemy to shame when we persevere through the trials and obstacles in our lives and in our congregations to continue the work God has given us to do.

We will put the enemy to shame when we speak to others with love and grace, focusing on the positive instead of dwelling on the negative.

We will put the enemy to shame when we encourage others in their walk, strengthen others in their faith, and support others on their journey of healing, restoration, and redemption.

In essence, we will put the enemy to shame when we LOVE!!

This week, remember that you have the power of the living Lord dwelling within you. As you fight through known and unknown battles this week, do so with God's love.

Confessions of the Pastor's Wife

Warrior God, help me to fight for you this week. Help me to love others.

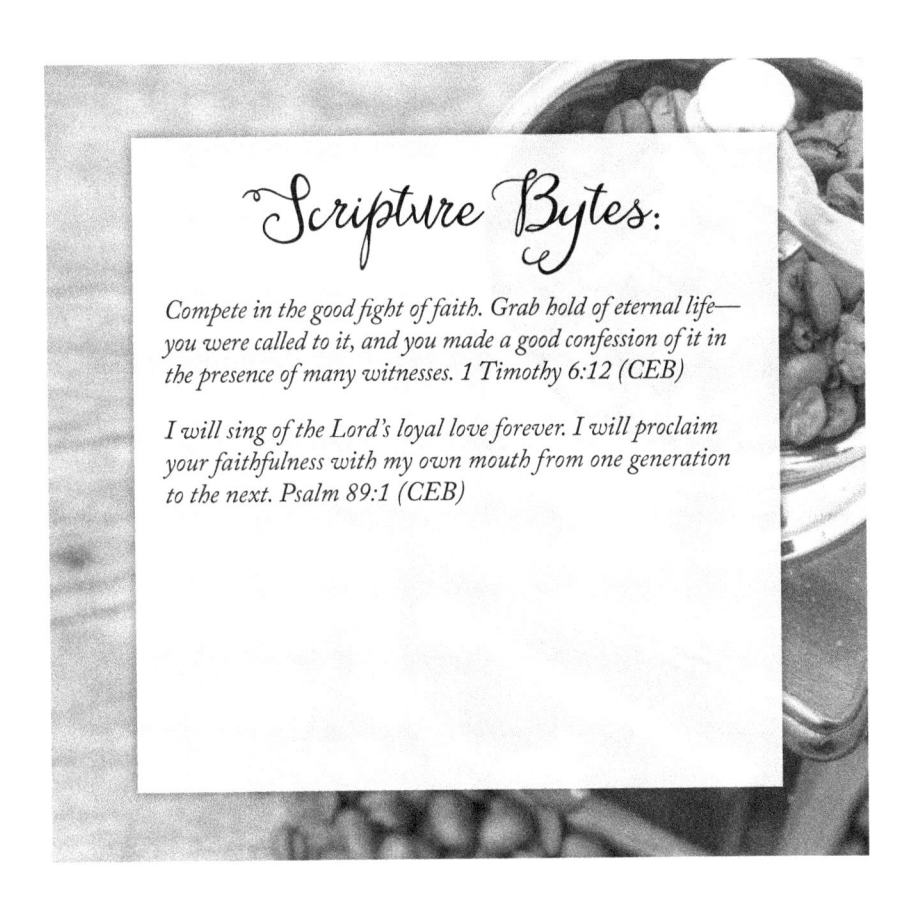

Scripture Bytes:

Compete in the good fight of faith. Grab hold of eternal life—you were called to it, and you made a good confession of it in the presence of many witnesses. 1 Timothy 6:12 (CEB)

I will sing of the Lord's loyal love forever. I will proclaim your faithfulness with my own mouth from one generation to the next. Psalm 89:1 (CEB)

Confessions of the Pastor's Wife

Confessions of the Pastor's Wife

PRAY

Is anyone among you in trouble? Let them pray! Is anyone happy? Let them sing songs of praise! Is anyone among you sick? Let them call the elders of the church to PRAY over them…Therefore, confess your sins to each other and PRAY for each other so that you may be healed. The prayer of a righteous person is POWERFUL and EFFECTIVE!!

James 5:13-16 (emphasis the author's) (NIV)

Each summer, our boys spend a week together at their grandparents' without Mom and Dad. It's a wonderful treat for both the kids and my husband and I. Even though the boys are hundreds of miles away, we stay connected. They call each evening and text throughout the day. One morning, I got a text from my youngest at about 7:30 a.m. It read:

Mommy, Grandma and I are walking and we just saw two bunnies. I love you.

Bunnies. My son was so excited about bunnies that he just had to text his mama early in the morning.

It made me wonder, how often do I do that with God? When was the last time I checked in with God just to tell him about the delight I found in his creation?

Umm…maybe…never…

Confessions of the Pastor's Wife

For too many of us, prayer takes a back seat to the other events or happenings in our lives. We bark orders at God or give a compulsory thanks before dinner, but we don't really spend time in conversation with the One who created us and knows us better than we know ourselves.

Did you know that psychologists have found that the healthiest relationships are the ones in which people engage in communication with one another at least four hours a day? (Don't worry, texting counts!) Think for a minute about the person you communicate most with throughout the day. Now, think about how much time you spend communicating with God throughout the day. Am I the only one whose numbers don't add up?

Communication is essential to a healthy relationship, and prayer in its most basic essence is communication. We go to God and talk and listen. It's a two-way conversation, even if we're not face to face. Yet even more importantly, prayer is our time to surrender ourselves to God. It is our time to go to God and tell him that we're ready for him in our lives—for his forgiveness, his love, his grace, his mercy, his peace, his strength, his guidance, his power, and his freedom.

Prayer is an essential component to our growth in God. And yet, so many of us are intimidated at the thought of spending too much time in prayer.

In our society, we over-complicate things. We make excuses to justify our lack of commitment to God and others. The solution to this is simple. To borrow a quote from my husband, "If you don't feel like you pray enough, then pray! If you don't feel like you read your Bible enough, read your Bible! If you feel guilty because you don't go to church enough, go to church! If you feel bad because you don't talk to your mom enough, call your mom!"

Confessions of the Pastor's Wife

There is no divine mystery to prayer. There is no special wireless connection or modem we need to activate. We don't need to use specific words or a specific template. We don't even need to be in church. We just need to be willing to open the door of our hearts and say, "Hey God, you wanna come in and talk for a bit?" We might be surprised to find that God is already there, waiting.

This week, take some time to strike up a conversation with God. Forget the prayer lists. Forget needing a certain time or place. Keep your eyes open and just talk to God. Tell him how you are. Tell him how you're feeling. Talk to him about what's been on your mind. Thank him for something beautiful or meaningful you experienced. Just talk, and then take a few more moments to listen. What is God saying to you in return?

Beautiful Savior and Redeemer, my heart is yours. Come in and speak to me this week.

Scripture Bytes:

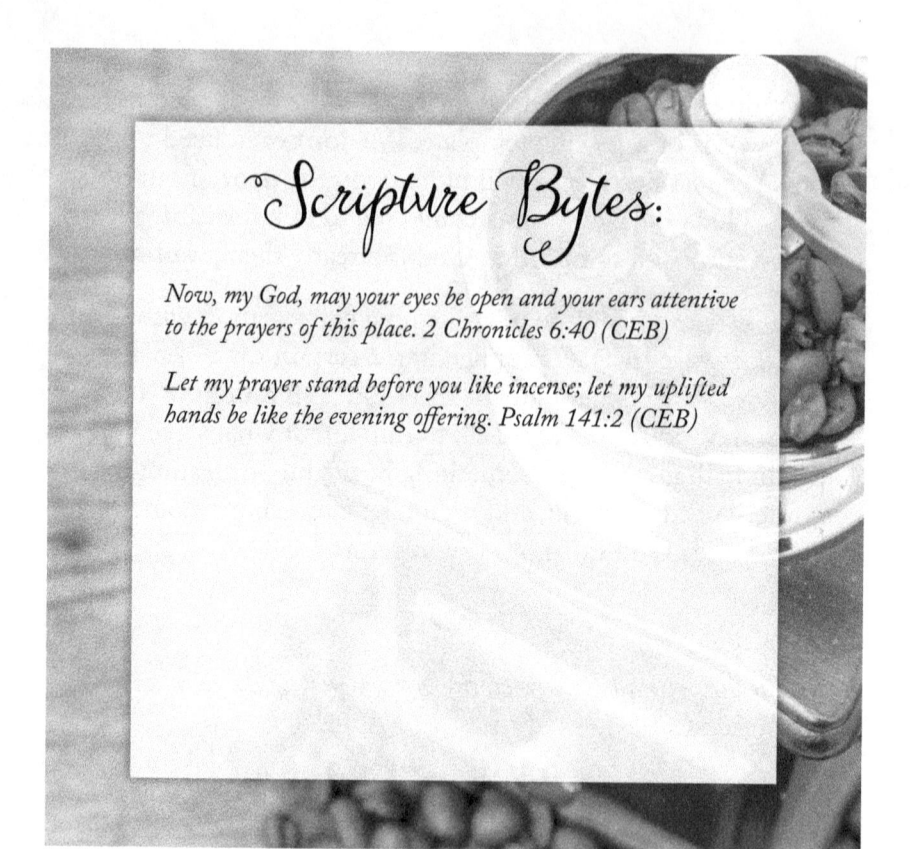

Now, my God, may your eyes be open and your ears attentive to the prayers of this place. 2 Chronicles 6:40 (CEB)

Let my prayer stand before you like incense; let my uplifted hands be like the evening offering. Psalm 141:2 (CEB)

Confessions of the Pastor's Wife

SINGLE-MINDED FOCUS

Focus your eyes straight ahead: keep your gaze on what is in front of you.

Proverbs 4:25 (CEB)

Having a very active imagination, my mind wanders a lot. Often when I'm cleaning or driving or trying to fall asleep, I make up stories in my head, little movies I can watch while I'm busy doing other things. Had I written them all down over the years, I would have filled hundreds of books! When I'm not making up stories I will probably never write, I am thinking about work I need to accomplish, running through a to-do list, worrying about the kids, or making plans for the next day. Often, my thoughts become muddled together due to my lack of focus.

Sometimes, my prayers get muddled too. Often, I ask God for help, advice, guidance, and direction, yet I do not clear my mind of other things to allow God's help, advice, guidance, and direction to come through. Romans 12:2 tells us that it is in the renewing of our minds that we will be able to discern God's will, yet, how do we renew our minds? How do we keep our eyes straight ahead?

Confessions of the Pastor's Wife

First, I think we have to clear our minds. We have to stop thinking and daydreaming and worrying, and allow stillness to permeate our being.

Next, when our minds are clear and still, we need to go to God's Word. We need to pour over Scripture, letting the words imprint themselves on our newly cleared minds. We need to soak in the Word of God, whether a chapter or two or just one verse.

Then, we need to ponder. We need to re-read our Scripture passage or verse. We need to read the commentaries about it, gather information around it, think about what it means in our own lives. We need to ask God for clarity about his Word.

Finally, we need to pay attention to Scripture lived out in our lives. Where is our passage meeting us throughout the day? Where are we living out the Word we have received? How is God illuminating it for us throughout our day?

I've found it beneficial to write a Scripture passage (or verse) on a sticky note and post it where I will see it often. This allows me to reflect on God's Word when I am brushing my teeth, washing my hands, working on my computer, driving in the car, making dinner, or even walking into the house.

When we take the time to focus on God, the road ahead becomes clearer. We live with greater purpose and meaning, because we are better able to discern God's will and feel his presence. Focusing on God helps us to see what is in front of us and to keep putting one foot in front of the other.

This week, take some time to really focus your thoughts on God. Clear your mind of all the myriad thoughts that get in the way to focus on the One who is holding a light in front of you.

Confessions of the Pastor's Wife

Holy God, help me to fix my gaze solidly on you. Help me to take hold of my thoughts and to focus them on you and your work in the world.

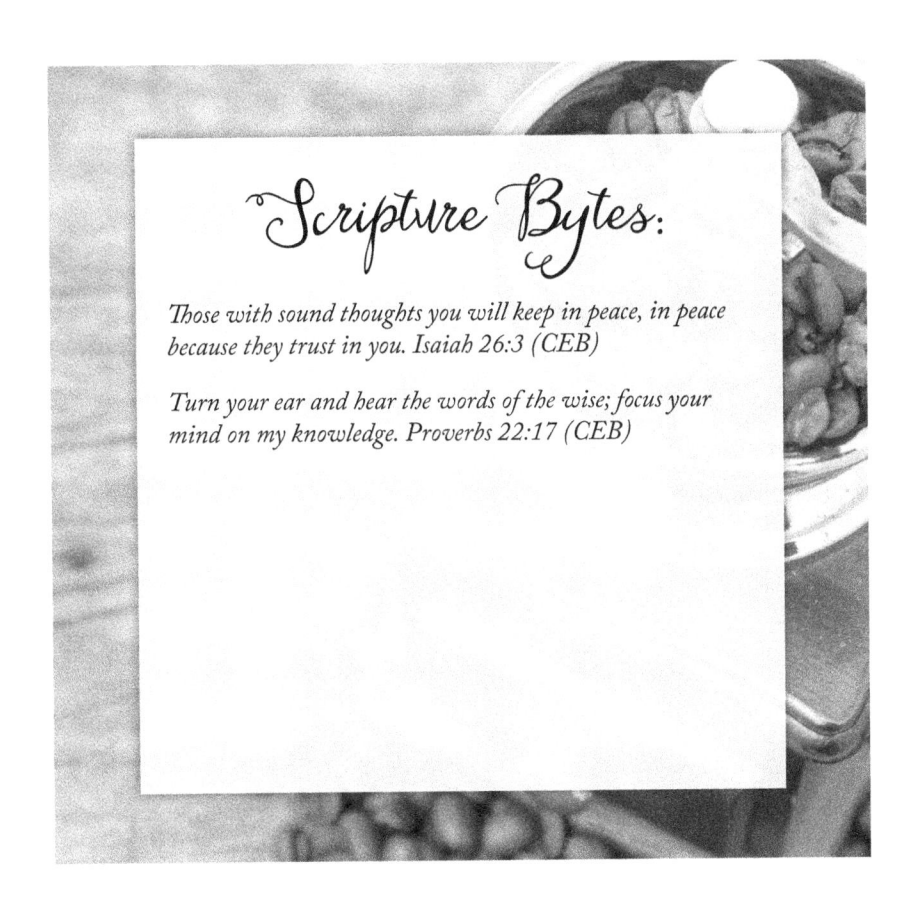

Scripture Bytes:

Those with sound thoughts you will keep in peace, in peace because they trust in you. Isaiah 26:3 (CEB)

Turn your ear and hear the words of the wise; focus your mind on my knowledge. Proverbs 22:17 (CEB)

Confessions of the Pastor's Wife

Confessions of the Pastor's Wife

I'M GOING WITH YOU

As Jesus walked alongside the Galilee Sea, he saw two brothers, Simon, who is called Peter, and Andrew, throwing fishing nets into the sea, because they were fishermen. "Come, follow me," he said, "and I'll show you how to fish for people."

Matthew 4:18-19 (CEB)

"Father, I don't know where you're going today, but I'm going with you."

Driving down the road, only half listening to the radio, these words from Sheila Walsh cut through my mental to-do list and planted themselves right in the center of my brain. It took me a moment to tune in to what I had heard, but as I rolled the words around in my head and let them drip onto my tongue, I realized the transforming potential of this small prayer. To begin each day with this is a lifestyle choice that requires some major shuffling of priorities for most of us. To-do lists might be left undone. Schedules carved into cyberspace might be deleted. Our five-year plan might not be there five years from now. Our agendas must be relinquished for God's agenda AND we have to choose to give them up willingly!

"Father, I don't know where you're going today, but I'm going with you."

Confessions of the Pastor's Wife

Can you imagine what the first disciples must have thought when Jesus called to them? Did Peter have any idea as he was folding away his fishing nets of the events to come? Peter, the rugged fisherman, who said "Father, I don't know where you're going today, but I'm going with you." Could he have known that he would become "The Rock" on which Christ would build his church, the first of the chosen twelve to recognize Jesus as the Son of God? Could he have foreseen his spectacular denial of Jesus, chronicled throughout time in all four Gospels, or had a vision of his own bloody death on a cross? If he had, do you think he would have gone? Would you? Would I?

"Father, I don't know where you're going today, but I'm going with you."

I think that this simple prayer embodies all we are to be as Christians. Our duty, our job, is to follow Christ. But look carefully at the words above—"Father, I DON'T KNOW where you are going...." To follow Christ, we have to be willing to take a leap of faith. We have to be willing to say, "I don't know" when it comes to the what, when, and where of our lives. We have to live on faith, that "confidence in what we hope for and assurance about what we do not see" (Hebrews 11:1). We have to remember that Jesus did not walk the easy road of comfort and luxury. Jesus sought out those who were poor, those who were sick, those who were oppressed, those who were weary, those who were "untouchable," and those who were "sinners." We have to remember that Jesus challenged the status quo. He pointed fingers at institutions (the government and the church), which kept people in bondage, which diminished the value and worth of human beings created in God's image.

"Father, I don't know where you're going today, but I'm going with you."

Confessions of the Pastor's Wife

Going with God involves taking risks. Jesus acknowledges to his disciples that the journey of discipleship will not only be hard, but there are few material or monetary rewards. But they went anyway. They took the risk because they understood that Jesus offered more than the world could hold. In order to go where God is going, we are called to take risks too.

Like Peter and Andrew, we might be asked to give up a career we have spent years training for. Like Abraham and Sarah, we might be asked to leave our comfortable homes and move to a new land. Like the young man looking for eternal life, we might be asked to give up our most valued possessions. Like Paul, we might be asked to cross cultural and social boundaries in order to share the love of God.

"Father, I don't know where you're going today, but I'm going with you."

This is what I want my prayer be. This is what I want my life to be. I want this prayer to be my lifestyle choice. I want to say to God, "I'M GOING WITH YOU!" wherever that may be. And even though the road may be difficult, I'm traveling with my Father. In what better place could I (could we) possibly be?

This week, make this prayer your prayer. Give each day to God, not knowing where his path might lead. Go with God, and see the wonder and joy and fulfillment a life spent following him can bring.

Father, I don't know where you're going today, but I'm going with you.

Confessions of the Pastor's Wife

Scripture Bytes:

As soon as they brought the boats to shore, they left everything and followed Jesus. Luke 5:11 (CEB)

But Ruth replied, "Don't urge me to abandon you, to turn back from following after you. Wherever you go, I will go; and wherever you stay, I will stay. Your people will be my people, and your God my God." Ruth 1: 16 (CEB)

Confessions of the Pastor's Wife

WHEN ENOUGH IS...ENOUGH

Elijah finally sat down under a solitary broom bush. He longed for his own death: "It's more than enough, Lord! Take my life because I'm no better than my ancestors." He lay down and slept under the solitary broom bush. Then suddenly a messenger tapped him and said to him, "Get up! Eat something!" Elijah opened his eyes and saw flatbread baked on glowing coals and a jar of water right by his head. He ate and drank, and then went back to sleep. The Lord's messenger returned a second time and tapped him. "Get up!" the messenger said. "Eat something, because you have a difficult road ahead of you."

1 Kings 19:4-7 (CEB)

Being the mother of two boys, life is always an adventure. My boys, like most kids, are busily creative, which is a nice way of saying they are crazy wild! A few years ago, our family moved into my parent's house for a week while foundation work was being done on our church parsonage. During that week, my boys seemed to have taken complete leave of their senses and left their ears back at our house. They were loud, destructive, mess-making creatures who brought chaos with them at every turn. While visiting my grandma in her assisted living facility one day, the boys were running up and down the halls and around the dining room, playing cars with Legos. My grandma, loving every minute, laughed and asked me, "Are they like this at home too?"

"ALL THE TIME! " was my response.

While my boys were generally pretty good, their change in routine had put them over the edge. Their wild moments became the norm and not the exception. I had had enough. While seriously considering leaving my boys on the nearest doorstep I could find, God spoke to me from the prophet Elijah.

In 1 Kings chapter 19, Elijah has had enough. After a spectacular defeat of the prophets of Baal on Mount Horeb, Queen Jezebel wants Elijah's head—literally. Having run from Queen Jezebel most of his career, Elijah is feeling like he's too old for this. He's tired. His energy is spent. He wants to be finished with his work. So Elijah flees into the desert looking for a quiet place to just get away from it all.

Elijah says to the Lord, "I have had ENOUGH, Lord!"

> *He lay down under the tree and fell asleep. All at once an angel touched him and said, "Get up and eat…" The angel of the Lord came back a second time and touched him and said, "Get up and eat, for the journey is too much for you" (1 Kings 19: 7).(NIV)*

Interestingly, or maybe I should say, "humanly," Elijah spoke those words to God shortly after God had displayed his power on Mount Carmel, exposing the priests of Baal as frauds and demonstrating once again to the nation of Israel that Yahweh is the one, true God. Yet instead of being full of confidence, of recognizing that he, Elijah, served the Most High God, Elijah took Jezebel's threat to end his life seriously and headed for the hills. Even though God had shown Elijah firsthand his power, his glory, his might, Elijah still said, "I have had ENOUGH!"

Confessions of the Pastor's Wife

The truth is, there are situations in all of our lives where we decide to tell God enough is enough, despite the ways God has sustained us in the past and our knowledge that he will do so in the future.

But here's what I love...instead of telling Elijah off, commanding him to get up and stop being a baby and get the job done, *God ministers to Elijah. God comforts Elijah. God sustains Elijah.* Do you see the love God has in his heart for his people? Do you feel the love God has for you? Elijah told God he had had enough and God responded with comfort and care, with empathy and compassion. God said, "I know this journey is too much for you, so let me see you through."

Have you recently told God you've had enough? I want you to know that God *knows* you've had enough. He *knows* this journey is too much for you. And he loves you with a love so great, so deep, so wide, so high that he is bringing you nourishment that will strengthen you, sustain you, and see you through!

Sustaining God, I have had enough. I'm tired and I'm worn. Like Elijah, I need rest. Please grant me your sustaining peace and comfort this week. Give me strength beyond my own to accomplish those tasks you have placed before me this week.

Scripture Bytes:

But look here: God is my helper; my Lord sustains my life.
Psalm 54:4 (CEB)

Our Lord Jesus Christ himself and God our Father loved us and through grace gave us eternal comfort and a good hope.
2 Thessalonians 2:16 (CEB)

Confessions of the Pastor's Wife

ABIDING IN SURRENDER

Moses said to them, "Wait while I listen for what the Lord will command concerning you."

Numbers 9:8 (CEB)

I am not a patient person. I don't like waiting, I like doing. When my oldest was three, he and I carpooled to school—he to a preschool and me to the high school where I taught. One morning, on the way to drop my son at school, I was stuck waiting on a red light. I waited, and waited, and waited…Finally, after two cycles of lights and no green arrow to turn left, I decided to take matters into my own hands. Looking both ways and seeing absolutely no other vehicle on the road, I made a left turn on a red light. Instantly, a little voice piped up from the backseat.

"Mommy, you went on a red light. You're not supposed to do that."

Grrr…why did he have to pay attention to everything? How could I tell my then three-year-old son that I was tired of waiting, and when you're tired of waiting, technicalities like stoplight laws just don't seem to matter? The truth is, waiting for something to happen can feel like surrendering. And, like many people, I equate surrender with giving up. Giving up is not in my nature. (However, as God is always quick to point out, perhaps I would be better off if it was.)

Surrender can be a bitter pill to swallow. Many of us go to a place of surrender with God only after life's circumstance throws a huge obstacle in our path we can't climb over, go around, dig under, or push through. We finally say, "That's it! I give up! You take it God." And then we stand back, hands on hips, catching our breath while we wait for God to vaporize it. And we wait, and wait, and wait. A few seconds stretch into minutes. We look each way, then crane our heads to the sky. Impatience begins to creep up from our feet, which are itching to get back on the path. The minutes continue on, but the obstacle is still in the path.

"Did you hear me?" we call to the sky. "Hello!" "Hello!?" "Hello?" Minutes stretch into hours, which bleed away the day. Darkness falls and we find ourselves asking, "God, where are you?" Days pass into weeks, months, even years. We've gone from a pup tent to pouring a foundation to a four bedroom, two-and-a-half bath house. And still we wait, surrendering again and again with each new day.

The reality of surrender is that sometimes God calls us to abide in it. These seasons of our lives living amidst obstacles we cannot budge are opportunities for God to demonstrate his power. But sometimes, the power he is demonstrating to us is his power to provide and care for us in the midst of our darkest hours. It is in these seasons that we learn the true nature of surrender. Surrender is not a one-time thing, but something we must do over and over with the dawn of each new day. Abiding in surrender.

We see this lesson taught over and over again in Scripture. Abraham waits and waits and waits for God to fulfill the

Confessions of the Pastor's Wife

promise of both land and children. He gets impatient, takes matters into his own hands, creates a huge mess, and must surrender all over again.

Joseph waits and waits and waits for God's salvation. He is thrown into a well, sold into slavery, and thrown into prison throughout the course of his story. At each stage of the journey, he must surrender to God.

Ruth and Naomi wait and wait and wait for God's redemption. They are widowed, impoverished, and childless. Ruth surrenders herself each day to the hard task of gleaning in the fields.

Paul waits and waits and waits for God's deliverance. Struck blind on the road to Damascus, Paul is forced to surrender himself to God's purposes. Once his vision is restored, Paul must surrender each new day on his long and difficult road of discipleship with God and trust in God's deliverance.

Our ability and willingness to surrender is important to God. But don't think for a moment that God is being mean, choosing to ignore a very real problem for the sake of disciplining his pig-headed children. While we are learning to abide in surrender, God is working on the other side of that obstacle, building a better road (toll-free!) for us to travel. He's straightening out the curves, adding extra lanes, re-paving, and re-painting. He's adding new road signs to help guide our path and creating new exits for us to take. God is working while we're abiding. Make no mistake about it, God can and will vaporize that obstacle blocking our path, but not before the road, and we, are ready!

The people of Israel wandered in the desert for forty years learning the lesson of surrender. While they traveled round and round in circles, God was hard at work. The people, his

Confessions of the Pastor's Wife

people, weren't ready for the next phase of the journey. They didn't understand who they were. They didn't understand Whose they were. The people needed this time in the desert to learn to become the people of God.

Sometimes, we need wilderness time too. We need to wander and wait, surrendering each day to God. It is in the surrender that we learn to trust and depend on God. When we surrender, we give God the green light to break into our lives, to break open our lives, and to transform our lives.

This week, take some time to surrender your life to God. Whatever obstacle is sitting squarely in the middle of your path, offer it up to God. Let it go. Give it to God. And trust that God is building a better path on the other side.

God, you are my salvation, my redeemer, and my deliverer. You know the obstacles that block my path. Help me to surrender them to you. Take my relationships, my work, my health, and my time. Help me to abide patiently in you.

Confessions of the Pastor's Wife

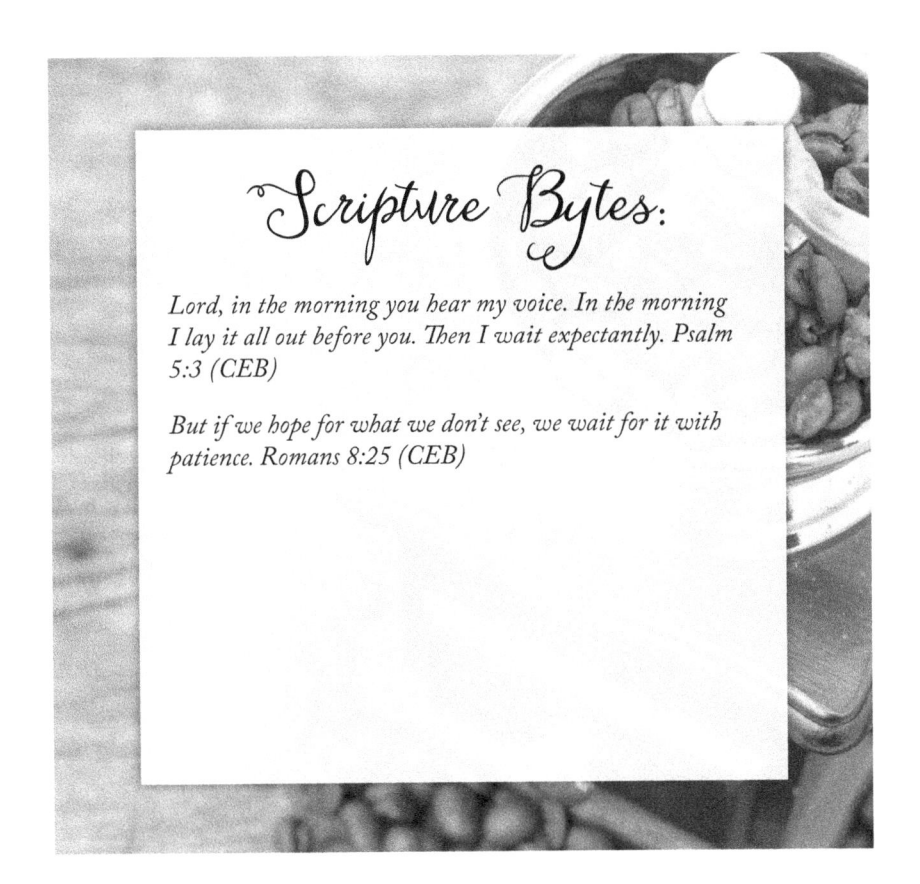

Scripture Bytes:

Lord, in the morning you hear my voice. In the morning I lay it all out before you. Then I wait expectantly. Psalm 5:3 (CEB)

But if we hope for what we don't see, we wait for it with patience. Romans 8:25 (CEB)

Confessions of the Pastor's Wife

Confessions of the Pastor's Wife

HOLDING TOGETHER

The Son is the image of the invisible God, the firstborn over all creation...He is before all things, and in him all things hold together.

Colossians 1:15, 17 (NIV)

When I was thirty-five, I had a pre-midlife crisis. My husband had been appointed to a new church in a very small rural community. Because we were moving some distance away from our previous church, I had to give up a beloved teaching position. The economy had tanked, teaching positions were hard to come by, and most rural districts were not interested in paying the salary of someone with a master's degree. I resigned myself to substitute teaching. I thought if I subbed for a year, then I could get my foot into the door of a local district and come away with a full-time contracted teaching position. Boy, was I wrong!

Entering into my second year without a contracted full-time job, I broke. I had interviewed for a job in which I thought God was opening a door, only to find it wasn't so. I had surrendered and re-surrendered to God's plan, but had no clear idea of what that plan might be. I was tired of pinching pennies and living paycheck to paycheck. I was tired of being unfulfilled. And yet, I learned a lot about myself and my priorities through this process.

Confessions of the Pastor's Wife

God taught me some good lessons about what was important. Furthermore, God provided for all of our NEEDS.

God was faithful and I tried to be so as well. Although that season of my life lasted a bit (lot) longer than I expected or desired, I knew God's plan would be revealed in HIS time. The pieces would all come together.

Colossians chapter 1 tells us that Jesus is the image of God, and that in him, all things hold together. John chapter 1 tells us that Jesus is the Word, that he was there in the beginning, and that through him all of creation took shape. Jesus, the Word, holds all things together.

I don't know what you're facing in your life right now, but in Colossians, Paul is clear that God's got it covered. So if you're feeling tired, overwhelmed, defeated, or anxious—if it seems like life is falling apart—take heart! God is holding it all together! And, unlike us, his hands are big enough to do it all! God is not going to drop the ball when it comes to our lives! Where we see one big mess, one impossible hurdle to overcome, God sees a master plan coming together. I love those t-shirts that say, "Work in Progress." I think I need that phrase stamped on my forehead! God is constantly working in our lives.

I had no idea of the incredible journey God was leading me down when I was struggling to find a job four years ago. I couldn't see the bigger picture. And the picture I had, the life I was hoping for, pales in comparison to what God has done and is still continuing to do. So hang on, my friends, through whatever struggles you are facing today. Hang on, knowing that God, through Christ, is holding it all together.

Confessions of the Pastor's Wife

God of infinite wisdom and understanding, thank you for holding all things together. Thank you for simply holding me. Grant me patience, trust, and hope as I journey this path. Let me see the big picture when I am ready.

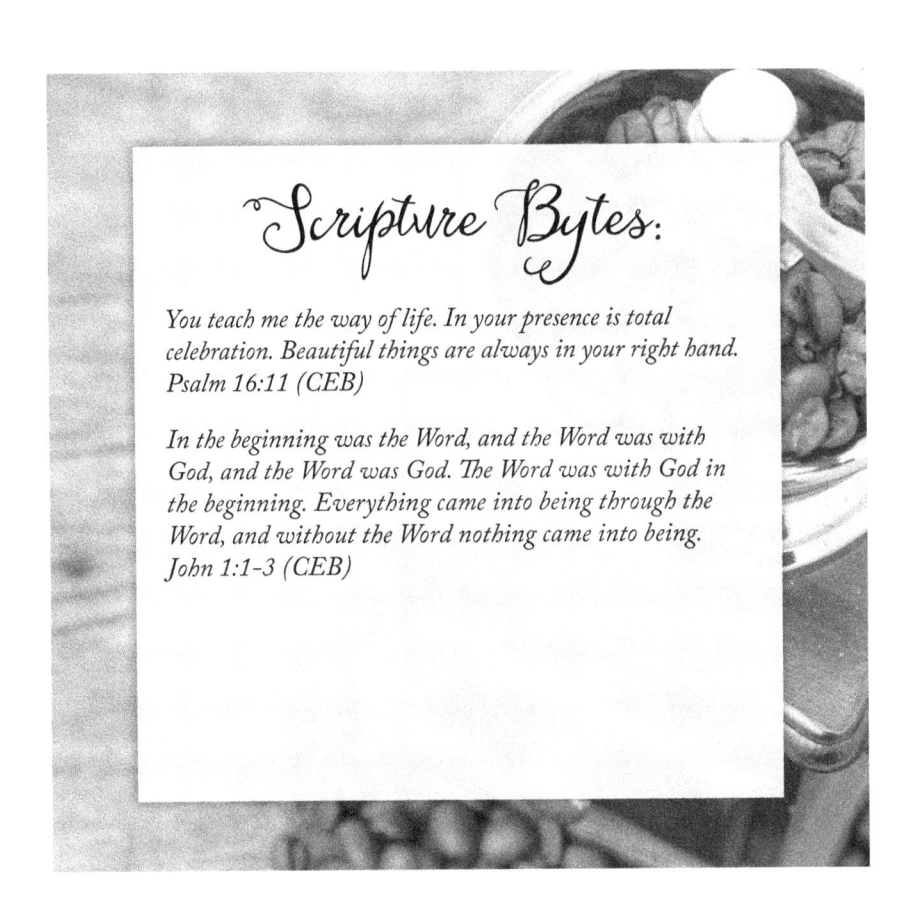

Scripture Bytes:

You teach me the way of life. In your presence is total celebration. Beautiful things are always in your right hand.
Psalm 16:11 (CEB)

In the beginning was the Word, and the Word was with God, and the Word was God. The Word was with God in the beginning. Everything came into being through the Word, and without the Word nothing came into being.
John 1:1-3 (CEB)

Confessions of the Pastor's Wife

Confessions of the Pastor's Wife

BE YOURSELF

Everything that has been created by God is good, and nothing that is received with thanksgiving should be rejected.

1 Timothy 4:4 (CEB)

"Just be yourself." How many times do we get that advice in our lives? People say that before a job interview, before a first date, when we move to a new place, begin a new career.... yet my problem is, I don't want to be myself. I want to be someone better. Throughout my life I have gotten caught up in the notion of who I should be rather than who God made me to be. I try to live my life the way that people I admire and look up to live theirs. Let me give you a few examples...

My best friend is the mom I have always wanted to be. She and her husband had an idea for the life they wanted to create with their family and they have done just that. She is wise and creative in her parenting. Her kids are smart, creative, inventive, and completely unique individuals. They've never been introduced to Pop-Tarts or chicken nuggets. Instead, they get home-made granola bars, freshly-grown vegetables out of the garden, and organic dairy and meat. I look at her life and think, "That's what I want to do!"

The problem? I'm not her.

Confessions of the Pastor's Wife

My sister is a force to be reckoned with. Strong, brave, and outspoken, she speaks her mind and makes a difference in the lives of those she works for and with. She doesn't back down to the challenges of life, but rather, bowls them over with her indomitable spirit. So many times in my life I have been in situations where I thought, "If I were Libby, I would just say..."

However, I am not Libby. I'm just me.

I could go on and on, but the sum of it all is this: God made ME. If he had wanted a carbon copy of my BFF or my sister, he would have made them. But he didn't. He made me. Trying to live my life like someone else is a waste of the precious time and talents God has entrusted me with here on earth. You see, God has a plan for *my life*, the same as he has a plan for yours. And he has placed within each of us all of the gifts we need to fulfill that purpose if we would just give ourselves over to him.

God tells us:

- I know the plans I have for YOU! (Jeremiah 29)
- I made you a mighty branch so that you might grow my fruit and bring it to the world. (John 15)
- I formed you in the image of my Son. (Romans 8)
- I formed you in the image of ME, that my purposes might be fulfilled in your life. (Ephesians 1)
- *I need you to be the person I created you to be.*

Talk about ultimate freedom! The truth is, we don't have to be the person we think we should be. Instead, we must strive to be the person God created us to be. We need to seek the purposes God would have for us, to let go of who we think we should be, and

Confessions of the Pastor's Wife

focus on who God designed and gifted us to be. This week, spend some time thinking about the gifts and abilities God has given you. How can you use those to engage in the work of God? How can you develop and strengthen those gifts and abilities so that you are comfortable just being yourself?

I don't know what the end result of my life will look like, but I'm going to "press on to take hold of that for which Christ Jesus took hold of me" (Philippians 3:12). (NIV)

Dear God, my Creator, thank you for loving me enough to make me the unique individual that I am. Thank you for the gifts and abilities you have bestowed upon me. Help me to see them for what they are and to use them in ministry for you.

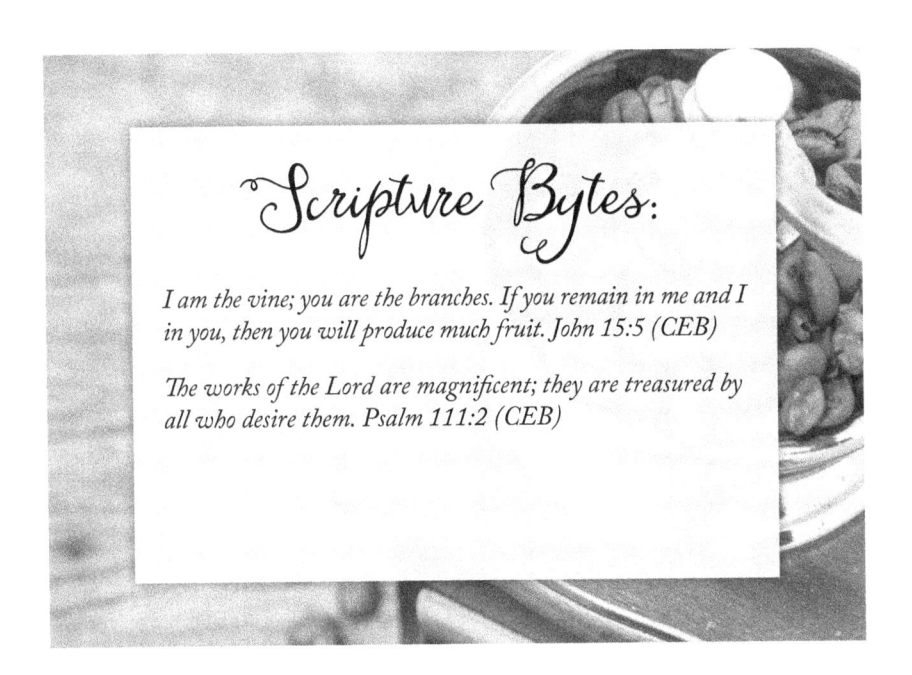

Scripture Bytes:

I am the vine; you are the branches. If you remain in me and I in you, then you will produce much fruit. John 15:5 (CEB)

The works of the Lord are magnificent; they are treasured by all who desire them. Psalm 111:2 (CEB)

Confessions of the Pastor's Wife

Confessions of the Pastor's Wife

ORDINARY TIME

There's a season for everything and a time for every matter under the heavens.

Ecclesiastes 3:1 (CEB)

I took down the Christmas tree yesterday. There was no real thought in the decision to do it. I was simply looking at it and realized that I was ready for it to be gone. My husband thinks, as much as he hates the trappings of Christmas, that the bareness from the decorations being gone is a bit sad, but I like it. It is winter and I am ready to abide in the sparseness of it. It is time to pull out the fleece blankets and hunker down.

This time of year in the liturgical calendar is referred to as Ordinary Time. Ordinary Time consists of the weeks surrounding Lent-Easter and Advent-Christmas. Typically, there are thirty-four weeks of Ordinary Time throughout the year. The color for Ordinary Time is green. Don't ask me why. Maybe green was an ordinary color for the Mediterranean men who created the church calendar. Personally, I would have chosen brown. And, while Ordinary Time does not have the pomp and circumstance of Christmas and Easter, it is the time in which we live out the majority of our lives. How ironic, then, that we would call it ordinary! The early church fathers were, of course, almost a full millennium before Thornton Wilder's Our Town in which the deceased heroine is granted one more precious "ordinary" day on Earth and cries out before departing, "Do any human beings ever realize life while they live it—every, every minute?"

The truth is that the Ordinary Time in our lives is, in fact, the sacred stuff life is made up of. Kathleen Kenison, in her book, The Gift of an Ordinary Day, refers to these moments as "charmed moments, all the time, in every life and in every day, if we are only awake enough to experience them when they come and wise enough to appreciate them."

It is the peaceful quiet that comes in the early morning or late night hours when you can hear the gentle breathing of your spouse, your children, and your pets gathered safely under one roof. It is the time spent together around a dinner table, noisy and rambunctious (as toddlers would rather play than eat), but time together, nonetheless. It is a deep breath of crisp winter air that expands the lungs and clears the head. It is a hot shower, it is the smell of warm yeast bread baking in the oven. It is time shared with friends and family to celebrate nothing except the fact that we enjoy one another's company. Our Ordinary Time is, perhaps, the most beautiful gift we are given in this life, and we should live each of our "ordinary" days in gratitude for it. We need to, as Kension writes, "pay attention to what's worth caring about, to read the sacred in everyday life."

Yet beyond our gratitude for our "ordinary" days, we must learn to live each one with the purpose for which it was intended. As the apostle Paul writes in Ephesians 2, "we are God's handiwork, created in Christ Jesus to do good works, which God prepared in advance for us to do" (NIV).

As the majority of our lives are lived in Ordinary Time, so the majority of our work to build the kingdom of God should be done in this time as well. It's easy to be generous at Christmas time, but is it as easy in March or August? And, are not these

Confessions of the Pastor's Wife

ordinary times the times that people need the most help, love, support, and care? As Christians, we need to take the gifts of our "ordinary" days and give them to those we meet along the way. They are simple gifts to give: gifts of presence, gifts of time, gifts of food, gifts of acknowledgment, gifts of comfort, gifts of encouragement, and gifts of love.

Ordinary Time is our time to realize life while we live it—every, every minute—and to share that life with those around us.

Eternal God, thank you for the gift of ordinary days. Help me to live them out with gratitude, appreciating every, every minute. Let me use this ordinary time to do extraordinary work for you.

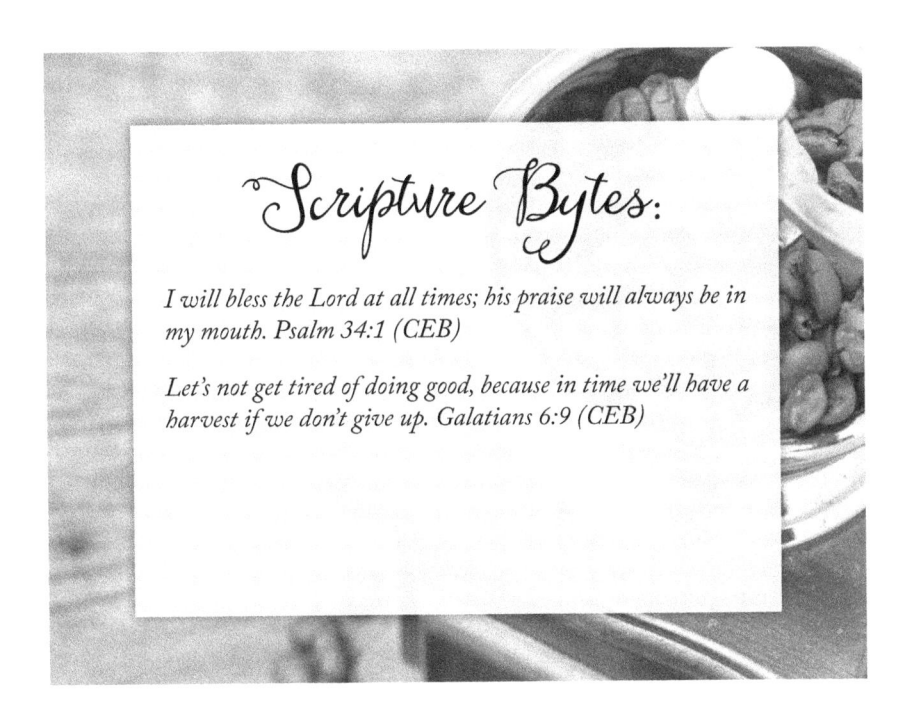

Scripture Bytes:

I will bless the Lord at all times; his praise will always be in my mouth. Psalm 34:1 (CEB)

Let's not get tired of doing good, because in time we'll have a harvest if we don't give up. Galatians 6:9 (CEB)

Confessions of the Pastor's Wife